Europe's Middle East Dilemma

Studies in International Politics

Leonard Davis Institute for International Relations,
The Hebrew University, Jerusalem

About the Book and Authors

Soon after the European Summit in 1969, when the member states of the European Economic Community first met to achieve "European political cooperation," the Middle East conflict was adopted as the first foreign policy issue around which to form a consensus. In this book, Drs. Greilsammer and Weiler analyze the principal landmarks in the evolution of a unified European stance toward the Middle East conflict, placing events in the context of the contemporary political and economic circumstances. Among the events they review are: the November 1973 declaration recognizing, for the first time, "the legitimate rights of the Palestinians"; the London declaration of June 1977 establishing the Palestinians' right to a homeland; and the Venice declaration of 1980 affirming the Palestinians' right to self-determination and the necessity of PLO participation in the peace process. Finally, the authors offer a theoretical scheme for the study of European political cooperation and consider the implications of a European foreign policy toward the Middle East independent of that of the United States.

Ilan Greilsammer is associate professor of comparative politics in the Department of Political Science, Bar-Ilan University, Israel. He is the author of books and articles on the process of European integration and European politics, including *Les fédéralistes européens en France depuis 1945* and *Israel et l'Europe*. **Joseph Weiler,** professor of European law at the University of Michigan Law School, has written books and articles on the law of the European Common Market, international law, and comparative law. He has just published *Israel and the Creation of a Palestinian State, A European Perspective.*

STUDIES IN INTERNATIONAL POLITICS
LEONARD DAVIS INSTITUTE FOR INTERNATIONAL RELATIONS
THE HEBREW UNIVERSITY, JERUSALEM

Europe's Middle East Dilemma: The Quest for a Unified Stance

Ilan Greilsammer
and Joseph Weiler

Westview Press • Boulder and London

Studies in International Politics, Leonard Davis Institute for International Relations, The Hebrew University, Jerusalem

This Westview softcover edition is printed on acid-free paper and bound in softcovers that carry the highest rating of the National Association of State Textbook Administrators, in consultation with the Association of American Publishers and the Book Manufacturers' Institute.

Published in 1987 in the United States of America by Westview Press, Inc.; Frederick A. Praeger, Publisher; 5500 Central Avenue, Boulder, Colorado 80301

Library of Congress Cataloging-in-Publication Data
Greilsammer, Ilan, 1948–
  Europe's Middle East dilemma.
  (Studies in international politics)
  Bibliography: p.
  Includes index.
  1. European Economic Community countries—Foreign
relations—Arab countries. 2. Arab countries—Foreign
relations—European Economic Community countries.
3. European Economic Community countries—Foreign
relations—Israel. 4. Israel—Foreign relations—
European Economic Community countries. 5. Jewish-Arab
relations—1973– . I. Weiler, Joseph, 1951– .
II. Title. III. Series: Studies in international
politics
DS63.2.E8G73 1987   327.4017′4927   86-32574
ISBN 0-8133-7359-X

Composition for this book originated with conversion of the authors' word-processor disks. This book was produced without formal editing by the publisher.

Printed and bound in the United States of America

The paper used in this publication meets the requirements of the American National Standard for Permanence of Paper for Printed Library Materials Z39.48-1984.

6   5   4   3   2   1

Contents

Preface

European involvement in the struggle between Palestinian and Jew over and in Israel is as old as the Arab-Israeli conflict itself. Long before the First World War, when the early Zionist activists and pioneers were making their way to Palestine, European states intervened, on occasion with considerable vigor, with the Ottoman authorities to remove restrictions on this immigration. To some extent there was a measure of European sympathy even in those days for the Zionist ideal. But neither this sympathy nor any humanitarian concern was the principal motivation for the action. As always in affairs of state—especially the old European states—self-interest was at the root of European involvement. Ottoman restrictions on the entry of European citizens into Palestine were a contravention of the capitulation system of privileges which the European states had secured for themselves, and this could not be tolerated.

The First World War and its aftermath are well-known chapters in the history of the region. The Sykes-Picot Agreement, the MacMahon Correspondence, the Balfour Declaration and the subsequent League of Nations Mandate—in all of which European states played a major part—were not of course the root causes of the conflict but they certainly had a cardinal role in conditioning its special character. In more recent times the European role has been no less pronounced. A prime example is the 1956 Suez Crisis, the last major event in which European powers assumed an important role. Indeed, 1956 is a turning point after which one can speak of a pronounced European withdrawal—perhaps even abdication—from the region.

A new direct European involvement emerged in the early 1970s, first timidly and then with some fanfare. The hallmarks of the new involvement were twofold. In content there was a move to what Europeans have called a more "balanced" approach to the region and the conflict; Israelis have characterized this more directly as a pro-Arab shift. In form and procedure the new policy was novel: the member states of the European Economic Community attempted, particularly in the context of the Arab-Israeli conflict, to promote and execute a *common* foreign policy, often encapsulated in the slogan "Europe speaking with one voice."

In our study we focus on this last episode in the European involvement in the region. On the one hand, ours is a traditional diplomatic history, telling the story of, and analyzing the forces which shaped, this new "common" policy. On the other hand, it is not only the external substantive dimension which is of interest to us. We are equally interested in the European experiment of evolving, or at least aspiring towards, a common foreign policy in the context of the ongoing process of European integration. Clearly, the institutional and procedural context in which the policy has been established has influenced its content and effect.

In other words, the Arab-Israeli conflict provides us with a concrete setting in which to assess the relative advantages and disadvantages, successes and failures, of a Europe speaking, and occasionally stammering, with one voice.

The organization of the study is a simple one. In the first chapter we analyze the evolution of the foreign relations apparatus of the European communities, emphasizing the emergence of the Framework for Political Cooperation, the instrument through which Europe has made its first attempts to create a "common" foreign policy. We juxtapose the European Framework with that of full-fledged federal states in order to supply a frame of reference for analysis and as a means for pinpointing the unique characteristics of the Community in this field. We try to highlight the complex, and at times conflicting, aims and objectives of the Community and to provide a conceptual basis for both understanding and evaluating the output of the Framework.

In the second and third chapters of the study—the heart of our work—we trace step-by-step the evolvement of the European policy, through the Framework for Political Cooperation towards the Arab-Israeli conflict in general and the Palestinian dimension in particular. The Venice Declaration of 1980 provides an historical and, as we shall see, also a conceptual turning point in the European approach. Chapter Two deals with events leading up to the declaration from the inception of the Framework for Political Cooperation, and Chapter Three examines the aftermath up to and including the war in Lebanon.

In the fourth and final chapter we try to combine the two principal themes of the study. Our overall conclusions regarding both the substantive external objectives of the European policy and its internal integrative effect are rather negative. We suggest that in relation to both dimensions the European success is rather modest. Although we offer some tentative explanations, one will need more historical distance for a definitive evaluation.

The Framework for Political Cooperation and its operation in the context of the Arab-Israeli conflict have not yet been the subject of extensive study. This has to a certain extent conditioned our mode of presentation. Our political-historical analysis is a relatively detailed one, reporting media and political reaction as well as the events themselves and our interpretation of them. Moreover, we reproduce throughout the study the verbatim texts of the principal pronouncements of the protagonists. This is important in itself since, as we shall see, much of the European "policy" has consisted of statements, and its evolution can be traced through the nuanced shifts in these statements. We hope that the reader may profit from having the original texts, which are not always readily available.

We have not of course eschewed the theoretical dimension of the subject. We try to give the reader some tools with which to understand and evaluate the new European policy. We have put our heads squarely on the chopping block by rejecting both descriptively and prescriptively the classical "One Voice" model or ideal-type against which to evaluate the Framework for Political Cooperation. In proposing in its stead a more complex pluralistic model we are confident that there will be no shortage of executioners. If nothing else, our analysis may inspire some reassessment of the European venture in this field.

Prof. Ilan Greilsammer wishes to express his deepest gratitude to the Avigdor Baor Fund (Bar-Ilan University) and the Avigdor Baor family, for the generous support extended to him in connection with his research in 1982–1985.

This work begun with a joint paper on the subject at the Amsterdam colloquium on "European Foreign Policy-Making and the Arab-Israeli Conflict" (February 1983). This study is a much expanded version of that paper, which has been published in a book edited by David Allen and Alfred Peijpers (The Hague: Martinus Nijhoff Publishers, 1984). We are of course indebted to the organizers and editors of that earlier venture for the inspiration which we drew from that stimulating occasion. We would like to thank Mr. Martin Westlake, who did extremely useful press archive work. Institutional thanks must go to the Department of Political Studies of Bar-Ilan University, the European University Institute, and the Jerusalem Center for Public Affairs, which provided the necessary research facilities.

Abstract

In this book the authors analyze the attempts by the member states of the European community to coordinate their foreign policies and formulate a unified stance with regard to the Arab-Israeli conflict.

In December 1969 at the European Summit at The Hague, marked by President Pompidou's and Chancellor Brandt's expressed wish to "relaunch" the process of European integration in the political sphere, the member states of the EEC decided to try to bring their foreign orientations closer to each other and achieve "European political cooperation." Starting in 1970 with the Davignon Report, that movement towards political cooperation gained momentum.

Later, when the Europeans decided to adopt the Middle East question as the first possible field for a common foreign policy, it was partly because the oil problem pressured them to satisfy the political demands of the Arab world, and partly because the Europeans' attitudes on the Israeli-Arab conflict had converged over the years. France's position, expressed at the time of the Six Day War by President de Gaulle, was now understood and even accepted by most European countries. Moreover, the Palestinian question became the focus of the world's interest.

The principal landmarks in the evolution of a European stance towards the Middle East were:

- The November 1973 declaration recognizing, for the first time, "the legitimate rights of the Palestinians";
- The London declaration of June 1977 recognizing that the Palestinians have "the right to a homeland"; and
- The Venice Declaration of 1980 affirming the Palestinians' right to self-determination, and the necessity of PLO participation in the peace process.

This book analyzes the circumstances in which those decisions were made as well as the content of these documents. It offers a theoretical scheme for the study of the process of European political cooperation and considers the conditions of the European community's formulating a foreign policy independent of the United States.

Ilan Greilsammer
Joseph Weiler

ONE

The Historical, Conceptual and Comparative Framework

The European Community is not a federal state nor does it aspire to become one. Like federal states, however, it is a *non-unitary* political and legal system. There is a constant tension between the central (general) power and the constituent units; a continuous interaction between centrifugal and centripetal forces. In order to understand better the European process it may be useful to contrast it to other non-unitary actors and in particular the federal state. Many of the problems which Europe faces in constructing mechanisms for a common foreign posture derive from her non-unitary character rather than simply from disagreement among the partners about the possible content of a foreign policy. And since in this chapter we are concerned with mechanisms and institutions rather than substance, it is useful to concentrate on this essential structural characteristic of the Community. Through the differences (and occasional similarities) with these other non-unitary actors we may gain insight into the very special and unprecedented nature of the European Community's foreign-policy apparatus.

Typically, in the history of most federal states, the international environment provided one of the cardinal incentives for initial unification, or for the movement from confederal arrangements to some form of federation.[1] And although constitutions of federal states, normally based on a doctrine of division of powers between central government and the constituent units, describe with greater or lesser detail the respective competences allocated to each level of government, ". . . it is usually assumed that the foreign relations of a federation will be controlled predominantly, if not exclusively, by the general government of the whole territory."[2] (This, as we shall see, contrasts sharply with the European Community where foreign policy was precisely that area which the integrating member states sought most jealously to exclude from the competences of the central Community organs.)

A useful prism through which to illustrate the point is provided by the manner in which states contract international treaties. The treaty-making experience is important since treaties are the principal means through which the EC conducts its external relations.

Let us examine first the collective experience of federal states which in fact demonstrates strong converging trends. The first issue concerns the question of international personality and capacity of member units of a federation. Can the member states of a federal state conduct an independent foreign policy? In many federations this power is denied constitutionally. Historically, even in federations such as the Federal Republic of Germany, Switzerland and to a certain measure the USA, where there is some constitutional provision for member-state international capacity, the actual exercise of this power is rare. In recent times member states have seldom concluded independent treaties and have preferred to rely on the federal government with, as in the FRG, certain constitutional guarantees.

For its part, public international law takes little cognizance of the internal structure of federations. Federal clauses (whereby other states recognize the internal federal character of a state) were always an inconvenient disturbance, at best tolerated and for the most part resisted, and both international capacity and international responsibility (the hallmarks of statehood and sovereignty) were accorded only grudgingly and to a progressively limited extent accorded to constituent units of federations. From the legal point of view the world order is composed of unitary actors.

Not surprisingly, the internal treaty-making power of the central government has been interpreted in most federal states in very broad terms. With a few theoretical exceptions the general trend is to recognize plenary treaty-making power limited by substantive constitutional provisions but not by allocational ones. In other words, in all federal states treaty-making power has not been limited to those areas over which the central government enjoys internal competences. And with the well-known exception of Canada and to a extent the Federal Republic of Germany, federal (central) governments have been allowed by constitutional courts to implement treaties even if the implementing legislation crosses the internal demarcation of competences. Court after court has ruled that the exigencies of the external environment may override the internal federal demarcation.

We see then, from the experience of federal states, that the conduct of foreign policy does not easily lend itself to non-unitary structures and that in this field the tendency—both in internal political terms and in the external international environment—is to opt for single actors. But how does this tendency square with the rationale behind federal arrangements—decentralization of power, participation, rational division of governmental powers among the participating units? Are foreign affairs to be excluded from this rationale and, if not, how does one explain the unitary tendency in federal states?

Even if federations have a unitary external posture, it is arguable that the federal principle may vindicate itself in the internal process of foreign policy-making. To be sure, the role of parliamentary organs at the central level in the foreign policy process, especially in the US (but not in the European Community) has increased dramatically in recent years by imposing a measure of democratic control on the foreign policy field, historically regarded as a *domaine reserve* of the executive. But it could be argued that federal legislative organs, even if designed to represent state interests have lost some of their mediatory function and have become part of the central authority—displaying less sensitivity and responsibility towards their original constituencies. Indeed, the process of foreign-policy making is for the most part not conceived as being a legitimate interest of the constituent units *qua* units of the federation.

We should note however that this unitarist image must be qualified, at least partially, by political fact. Across the board we find that even where federal govenments have the authority to encroach upon member-state competences through the exercise of treaty-making power, they have been very reluctant to conclude treaties which would have that effect. Moreover, there is a growing trend to evolve structures of cooperative federalism in order to overcome some of the problems posed by the unitary system. It remains true, however, that in the strict constitutional/international legal sense, federal states face the world as unitary actors and their internal policy process is essentially centralized.

We have still been unable to explain why, in the federal state which is based on a concept of division of competences, such exclusive power is allowed to rest in the hands of central government. The answer, we believe, must be found in the origins of the federal state.

Historically, the rationale behind this exclusive concentration of foreign affairs powers in the hands of the central government rested on three premises.

The first premise was that in matters of external relations a united posture would maximize the power of the individual units. This was especially the case in the areas of defense and security. One can go even further. The unified foreign posture and international personality emerged as probably the most important factors in giving federations in their formative years the quality of statehood, in contrast to other federal arrangements, such as confederations. This was certainly true in the formal relations among actors in the world order and was recognized in public international law.[3] But a unified foreign and defense posture did not have only an external and formal significance. The federation's flag, the federal army, the national anthem and other such paraphernalia— were all, at least in part, expressions of the unified posture towards "outsiders"—imbued the formal distinction with internal social meaning. Thus even at the social and human level, while citizens of a federation in internal matters could regard themselves as Texans or Tasmanians, vis-à-vis the outside world they would normally view themselves as Americans or Australians. *To be a federal state was to have a unified foreign posture.*

But this premise alone would not explain the willingness of the member states of federations—especially in formative periods in which there was traditionally much stronger insistence than today on preserving the rights and autonomy of the constituent units—to vest the execution of virtually all foreign power in the hands of the central government.

It is here that the second premise comes into play. For there was a widespread belief that matters of foreign policy and contacts with foreign states would, *ipso facto*, interest the general government and would be less relevant to the constituent states and the domestic powers usually vested in them.[4] It seemed therefore that one could benefit from a unified foreign posture without encroaching upon the internal division of powers between the two levels of government regarding domestic policy.

It is this premise which explains why, until the advent of the European Community, there was, with few exceptions, no such thing as a genuine "federal foreign policy."[5] Federal states distinguished themselves by their unified, *non-federal*, external relations.

Finally, perhaps there was the belief, characteristic of early federal theory, that the representation of state interests within federal government would sufficiently protect those interests—if indeed they existed.

Let us now critically examine these premises and their ramifications. The first premise which states that a united posture is more effective than individual foreign policies has retained much of its force until this day and constitutes the principal impetus for those who advocate further integration in the external posture of the EEC. By contrast, it is doubtful if the second premise was ever wholly correct.[6] And in today's inter-dependent world it is clear that there are few areas of so-called domestic jurisdiction which do not have some international dimension, and equally few areas of international activity which do not have internal ramifications.[7]

We are now in a position to understand the evolutionary dialectics and conceptual framework of the foreign relations apparatus of the EEC. The emergence of European institutions and mechanisms for the formulation and conduct of a common external posture was not a result of a preconceived and rational design. It was instead the outcome of a process conditioned by conflicting interests and forces.

On the one hand, the belief in the alleged benefits of having a unified foreign posture, of "speaking with one voice," at least in some contexts, provided the member states with integrative impetus. Moreover, the fact that internal matters tend to have an international dimension meant that even in areas where the Community was not vested with explicit external competence, there was pressure to create such competence so as to enable the EEC to pursue in an adequate manner its internal policies.[8]

On the other hand, it is easy to understand the source of member state ambivalence and resistance to a unified foreign policy. The very fact that a unitary external posture and single international personality emerged historically as the hallmarks of the federal state—distinguishing it from other non-unitary entities—was and remains a potent potion, perhaps even poison, for the member states. Even those who were most integration-minded did not call for the creation of a European "super-state," under whatever federal nomenclature. The area of foreign relations thus acquired a sensitivity unparalleled in any other field.

Furthermore, the patent falsity of the second premise, that one can delimit the interaction of internal and external powers, means that were the member states to vest the *exclusive* conduct of foreign policy in Community institutions they would not only lose their much cherished international personality, but would also be unable to autonomously conduct national policy in areas which at first might appear to be wholly within domestic jurisdiction. The history of all federal states has demonstrated clearly that implementation by federal government of federal foreign policy involves inevitable encroachment upon the areas reserved for states.[9]

Given then these conflicting interests we should not be surprised to find that all activities of the Community in the international environment are imbued with a strong ambivalence on the part of the member states. The potential external utility of the joint posture is always weighed against the alleged individual state's loss of power. The member states often want the substantive "benefits" but don't wish to pay the structural "costs."

We shall analyze first the initial pattern and evolution of the Community posture in the field of external economic relations, and then develop more fully the structure and purpose of its political foreign posture through the Framework for Political Cooperation. Finally, in this chapter we shall indicate the breakdown between the two external activity areas and reflect on a conceptual and evaluative framework into which the external posture may be fitted. We shall then be able to approach the central theme of this volume—European policy towards the Arab-Israeli conflict.

The Treaty Framework—
The External Relations of the EEC

The Starting Point

The EEC was created in 1958 against the backdrop of the more ambitious proposals in the mid-fifties for European political and defense communities. European integration was to evolve principally on the economic plane. The reluctance of the member states to extend their joint venture to defense (outside the NATO framework) and to foreign policy was reflected in two ways in the Treaty of Rome, which established the Community.

First, an "iron curtain" was drawn between what later became known as "high" and "low" politics. The Community was to have international competence only in respect to *external (economic) relations* (low politics). The member states would retain in their individual capacity exclusive competence over *foreign affairs* (high politics). There thus were a series of European commercial and trade agreements with many countries, including Israel, commencing already in the early sixties.[10] However, there could not be—until the creation of the Framework for Political Cooperation in the late sixties—even the semblance of a joint European policy towards the political issues besetting the region. Here one would have to have a French policy, a Dutch policy and so forth.

Anticipating a theme to which we may return later, this very example illustrates the untenability of a conceptual and operational distinction between high and low politics—between external relations and political cooperation. For one has to be singularly blind and dogmatic to believe that external economic relations operate in a political vacuum and that one can pursue a vigorous foreign policy without recourse to economic instruments.[11] The member states were to learn that lesson slowly and reluctantly. The theoretical division, so neatly drawn in the treaties which established the Community, was to become slowly unworkable, despite its ideological attraction.

Second, even in the realm of external relations the international capacity of the Community, expressed in particular through its treaty-making power, was explicitly granted only in relation to the international trade policy of the Community. Thus the treaty provides:

> The common commercial policy shall be based on uniform principles, particularly in regard to changes in tariff rates, the conclusion of tariff and trade agreements. . . .[12]

The treaty did use fairly general terms in allowing the Community to negotiate association agreements:

> The Community may conclude with a third State, a union of States or an international organization agreements establishing an association involving reciprocal rights and obligations, common action and special procedures. . . .[13]

But despite this broad language, when association agreements covered matters which could not be regarded as part of international trade, the member states prevented the Community from concluding such agreements alone and insisted on joint participation. Here as well, the untenability of the initial document is evident. Could the Community which had explicit, at times even exclusive, competence over matters such as fisheries and transport, operate as if the Europe of the Six (and later Nine and Ten) were a planet with no connections with third states and other international actors? Could there be a Community fisheries policy without Community agreements (treaties) with other fishing nations sharing the same seas?

Mutation of the Starting Point

For these and other reasons it was not long before the original treaty formulae were subjected to powerful mutations. The pattern of external relations today is a far cry from the initial blueprint. A telling example is the field of external economic relations. The number of external contacts of the Community which were formalized through international agreements has grown and runs into the hundreds. The Community also has an equally impressive network of international contacts through legations.[14] Any expectation that the external relations of the Community could or would be contained was inevitably proved false.

This growth was and is connected to two constitutional changes effected by decisions of the European Community Court of Justice. In a landmark decision of 1971 the Court broadened its interpretation of the Community's treaty-making powers and hence of its ability to engage in international affairs.[15] The Court held first that:

> In its external relations the Community enjoys the capacity to establish contractual links with third countries over the whole field of objectives defined in Part One of the Treaty. . . .

It added:

Such authority arises not only from an express conferment by the Treaty—as is the case with Articles 113 and 114 for tariff and trade agreements . . . but may equally flow from other provisions of the Treaty and from measures adopted, within the framework of those provisions, by the Community institutions.

Thus the treaty-making power of the Community would extend to all areas in which the Community had internal power. The confinement of Community agreements to international commerce and trade was removed.

In another development the Court, in the so-called *Ubber Case*, gave an extremely wide interpretation to the reach of the Community's common commercial policy. This was significant since according to this policy the Community was not only entitled to conclude agreements but had exclusive competence vis-à-vis the member states.[16]

Specifically the Court held:

It is . . . not possible to lay down, for Article 113 of the EEC Treaty, an interpretation the effect of which would be to restrict the common commercial policy to the use of instruments intended to have an effect only on the traditional aspects of external trade to the exclusion of more highly developed mechanisms. . . .

The same conclusion may be deduced from the fact that the enumeration in Article 113 of the subjects covered by commercial policy (changes in tariff rates, the conclusion of tariff and trade agreements, the achievement of uniformity in measures of liberalization, export policy and measures to protect trade) is conceived as a non-exhaustive enumeration which must not, as such, close the door to the application in a Community context of any other process intended to regulate external trade.

These developments could at first glance suggest a process not unlike that which occurred in most federal states—a monopolization of external contacts by, and a concentration of treaty-making power in the hands of, the central government. However, the very institutional structure of the Community and its political process render any such conclusion invalid. In particular we can mention two significant factors.

First, we must remember that the above process of expansion was confined to areas of external economic relations however widely defined. Explicit problems of defense, for example, and other issues of foreign affairs in the classical sense remained entirely in the hands of the member states.

Second, the member states reacted to the increased margin of competence of the Community to engage in external relations by tightening their grip on the actual procedures of treaty making, negotiating and implementation. It must never be forgotten that the central legislative/ decisional body of the Community—the Council of Ministers and its sub-organs—consists of representatives of the state governments. As such it was able over the years to reduce the autonomous role of the Commission in the external relations process in all its phases.

Although Article 228 and Article 113 explicitly state that negotiations of Community agreements were to be in the hands of the (supranational) Commission, and that only the final conclusion of the agreements would be delegated to the (intergovernmental) Council of Ministers, the member states were able to emasculate this provision. They did this by insisting that a seemingly innocuous sub-committee of the Council established by the treaty to assist the Commission in negotiations would in fact hold the latter to a mere plenipotentiary status. In addition, the demand that prospective Community agreements be concluded on a mixed basis— by the Community and the member states together— ensured automatic member-state representation at the negotiation phase.

Thus, although the external and internal environment forced the Community to assume an expanded external economic posture, the process of its execution moved away from a "supranational" centralized model to a more classical intergovernmental one. As Community external relations grew so did the role of the member states within this process. This has been a constant feature of almost all Community activity.

The Emergence of the Framework for Political Cooperation[17]

The Starting Point

While Community activity in the field of external economic relations found its basis in the treaties themselves, foreign policy proper (high politics) was, as we have seen, excluded from the Community process. The creation of the Framework for Political Cooperation as a mechanism for joint European activity in this area might therefore seem a process distinct and even detached from the internal Community processes described above. Although this is the classical view taken in the literature, our perspective is that a closer study will reveal that the same forces which shaped the evolution of external relations mechanisms conditioned the development of political cooperation.

There was a multiple rationale for the creation of the Framework. The "objective" reason was of course rooted in the claim that given the actual state of internal European integration, the failure to operate in the field of foreign policy was a waste of a significant potential. In other words, the argument was that a common European foreign policy would be able to project onto the world environment the joint power of the partners, a power that was greater than the sum of the individual units. A Europe which would *act* and *react* as a single actor to world events would according to this vision, be more effective than it had been in the past.

There was also an internal "subjective" reason. In 1969 the Community was emerging from a period of sustained political stagnation associated with de Gaulle's long term in office, and was recovering from the immediate after-effects of the Luxemburg crisis.[18]

The Community was to be "relaunched"[19] and together with the decision to accept the three new member states (Great Britain, Ireland and Denmark), concrete political initiative was the plan to set up the Framework for Political Cooperation. We may call this second reasoning the "reflexive" function of European political cooperation; the aim here was to find new areas in which Europe could manifest her newly found (and short-lived) "political will" as a sign of progress and hope.

While both the objective and subjective rationales pointed towards a rosy future for the Framework for Political Cooperation, in reality already at its inception there were powerful countervailing forces. Recalling our brief account of the evolution of external relations, it should come as no surprise that the first important steps in the evolution of political cooperation coincided with the institutionalized strengthening of the intergovernmental component in the European Community: the creation of the European Council of Heads of State and Government. This appears to be an almost constant factor in the mature phases of European integration: substantive progress is bought at the price of a decline in the unique decisional characteristics of the Community.[20] In this case the equation was at its extreme; the Framework for Political Cooperation was to be completely outside the treaties. It was not sufficient that in the Community of the seventies in which the Luxemburg Accord was an accepted way of life, the decisional process was completely dominated by the intergovernmental Council of Ministers, often at the constitutional expense of the Commission. For political cooperation, at least as initially conceived, any EEC contact was considered anathema. The European political cooperation institutions and procedures were thus to be insulated from any "contaminating" European Community contact. In a famous incident, typical of those early "watertight" days, the foreign ministers of the Community were forced to end a meeting in Copenhagen wearing one hat, and travel to Brussels in order to discuss the affairs of the Framework for Political Cooperation.[21] The Commission was emarginated from the political cooperation procedures or, at best, barely tolerated.

It is telling that the only Community organ which had an official role in political cooperation was the European Parliament. But not only did the Parliament have virtually no impact on the Community, especially before it was elected directly; its role in political cooperation was extremely limited as well.[22] This separation, symptomatic of the contradiction inherent in the process of European integration, was reflected in the very definition of the objectives of the Framework.

The Establishment and
Initial Evolution of the Framework

At the December 1969 Hague summit, the Heads of State and Government launched the idea of the Framework for Political Cooperation by agreeing:

> [T]o instruct the Ministers for Foreign Affairs to study the best way of achieving progress in the matter of political unification. . . . The Ministers would be expected to report before the end of July 1970.

The result was the October 1970 Luxemburg Report. Later we shall see the mechanisms of the Framework for Political Cooperation, but we should note here the cautiousness with which the objectives are expressed. Thus the ministers formulated the following goals:

> [T]o ensure, through regular exchanges of information and consultations, a better mutual understanding on the great international problems;

> [T]o strengthen [member state] solidarity by promoting the harmonization of their views, the co-ordination of the positions, and where it appears possible and desirable, common actions.

The language is extremely cautious, the objectives limited and the discrepancy between the high aspiration of the 1969 Hague summit— full economic and monetary European union within a decade—and the grim realism of the ministers very marked. The operational details set up by the Luxemburg Report were not far-reaching. The Framework for Political Cooperation was to be non-organic. It would depend on its activities on the co-ordinated apparatus of the member states—ministerial meetings and the like—and was to be outside the EEC framework. Thus the Report provided drily:

> Should the work of [the Framework for Political Cooperation] affect the activities of the European Communities, the Commission will be invited to make known its views.

In the 1972 Paris summit, the Heads of State and Government endorsed the creation of the Framework. Indeed they sought to improve it by increasing the frequency of meetings among the foreign ministers and linking the Framework to the EEC. In the language of the final communique:

> They considered that the aim of their co-operation was to deal with problems of current interest and, where possible, to formulate common medium and long-term positions, keeping in mind, *inter alia* the international political implications for and effects of Community policies under construction.

Interestingly, the idea of common action is played down; by contrast, the relevance of the Community is spelled out more clearly than it was in the past. The Framework for Political Cooperation was consolidated in the July 1973 second Ministerial Copenhagen Report. Beyond the self-congratulatory rhetoric of this report there were several significant points. Although the basic objective remained the same, the operational machinery was strengthened and in most important aspects became the foundation of the Framework. Significantly, each member state pledged:

> [A]s a general rule not to take up final positions [on common European foreign policy problems—however these may be defined] without prior consultation with its partners within the Framework of the Political Co-operation machinery.

The linkage to the Community was made more explicit even though the report insisted on the principled distinction between the Framework and the Community. We can only mention in passing a point to which we shall return in detail in subsequent chapters: the test of the Framework for Political Cooperation as consolidated by the Copenhagen Report was to come more rapidly than the ministers had envisaged with the outbreak of the Yom Kippur War in October 1973. The Framework proved totally inadequate to deal with the situation and Europe demonstrated a shameful display of disunity and individual member state self-interest. As we shall analyze below, and return to in our evaluative conclusion, the Framework did provide a useful mechanism for an orderly capitulation to the Arab oil interest.

If we skip ahead thirteen years from the first Luxemburg Report to the most recent Solemn Declaration on European Union[23] signed in Stuttgart in June 1983, we shall find that there have been no *dramatic* changes in the objectives of the Framework for Political Cooperation. The member states acknowledge:

[I]ncreasing problems of international politics [render] necessary [the] reinforcement of European Political Cooperation.

And yet despite this acknowledgement the new formulation of the objectives of the Framework underscores the inherent ambivalence and contradiction in the notion of a European foreign policy. It is worth citing the new formulation *in extensu*. The Solemn Declaration defines the following measures:

[I]ntensified consultations with a view to permitting timely joint action on all major foreign policy questions of interest to the Ten as a whole.

Prior consultation with the other member states in advance of the adoption of final positions. . . . The [member states] underline their undertaking that each . . . will take full account of the positions of its partners and give due weight to the adoption and implementation of common European positions when working out national positions and taking national action.

Development and extension of the practice by which the views of the Ten are defined and consolidated in the form of common positions which then constitute a central point of reference for member state policy.

Coordination of positions of member states on the political and economic aspects of security.

Increased contacts with third countries in order to give the Ten greater weight as an interlocutor in the foreign policy field.

Closer cooperation in diplomatic and administrative matters between the missions of the Ten in third countries.

The search for common positions at major international conferences attended by one or more of the Ten and covering questions dealt with in Political Cooperation.

It is clear thus that one is not speaking here of a single policy, with a single policy-making apparatus and a single policy-execution apparatus. The objectives of the Framework are in fact inherent in its name: political cooperation. The major actors remain the member states. Where the interest exists joint action would be encouraged, facilitated by the Framework mechanisms. Even the formulation of a common position, the nucleus of the Framework, is to serve only as a basis and reference point for national foreign policy. To underline this one can cite the Greek "reservation" at the time of signing the Solemn Declaration:

[I]n signing this declaration Greece states that nothing may restrain its right to determine its foreign policy in accordance with its national interests.

In many ways then, political cooperation as initially conceived was the story of the mountain which turned out to be a molehill. However, as in the case of external relations, the dynamics of the international environment as well as internal political pressures forced certain mutations in the original Framework. The result is still a far cry from a Europe speaking, let alone acting, with one voice. And even today, five years after it was written, the sober conclusion of von den Gablentz is still true: the Framework for Political Cooperation constitutes " . . . the world's most advanced model of collective diplomacy . . . [but] . . . neither the Community nor the [Ten] seem to have managed to perform the essential task of any foreign policy, namely to convert internal strength and resources into external influence on world affairs."[24]

How the Framework for Political Cooperation Works[25]

For our purposes a detailed description of the Framework is not necessary and a brief resume will be sufficient. Since launching the Framework in the summit of 1969 the institutional aspects of political cooperation have been revised several times, resulting in the following pattern of institutions and mechanisms.[26]

At the apex of the institutional framework stands the European Council of Heads of States and Government which since 1974 has represented formalization of irregular meetings which characterized Community life since the early Sixties. The European Council, itself an organ, strictly speaking, outside the Treaty framework,[27] is thus the ultimate forum for coordination of, and pronouncements on, foreign policy issues. The European Council can debate lower issues by its own motion and/or on the recommendation of the lower tiers of the Framework.

At the formal head of the Framework stand the foreign ministers who constitute the mainstay of the Framework. They meet at least 4 times a year and in reality far more frequently. Their formal forum is the conference of the Foreign Affairs Ministers meeting on European political cooperation matters. Their function is both constitutive—they may issue declarations in the name of the Framework—and preparatory—they lay the groundwork for meetings of the Heads of State and Government.

A political committee (the Daignon Committee), consisting of the directors of political affairs in the ten foreign ministries, meets regularly and serves as the main continuous preparatory forum for the political bodies of the Framework for Political Cooperation. A possible parallel within the Community bureaucracy would be the COREPER (Comite des Representants Permanents), which prepares the Council of Ministers' meetings. Although the Political Committee provides a measure of continuity transcending, for example, political change of office in any one of the member states, the Framework for Political Cooperation has no permanent secretariat despite the frequent calls to establish one. The Presidency of Political Cooperation moves with the Presidency of the Community at six month intervals and the only improvement to the disruption inherent in this modality has been the tripartite model whereby the current, previous and future presidencies meet in a coordinative forum.[28]

Working groups may be set up to study specific issues and they, in turn, may appoint groups of experts. The latter do not have an independent existence and they are strictly issue or region-oriented.

A "Group of Correspondents" in the various foreign ministries has been set up. They are the Framework for Political Cooperation "desk" in each capital and their task extends also to monitoring and following up political cooperation decisions and declarations.

Embassies of the Ten are associated within the Framework with a view to a two-way coordination with the European center. Likewise, the member state representations within international organizations, especially the UN, have the same association. The ambassadorial contacts become important in times of crisis, such as the Iranian affair. A special Telex system, COREU, which is used to handle the communication traffic of the Framework, carries a significant amount of communications.

In the recent 1981 London Report, the foreign ministers "codified" their procedures. The report proposes changes in the operational side of the Framework (such as better preparation of ministerial meetings) and a better defined role for the rotating presidency as the spokesman of the Ten. The most noticeable improvement has been the establishment of crisis procedures:

> The Political Committee or, if necessary, a ministerial meeting will convene within forty-eight hours at the request of three member states.

> The same procedure will apply in third countries at the level of Heads of Mission.

> In order to improve the capacity of the Ten to react in an emergency, working groups are encouraged to analyze areas of potential crisis and to prepare a range of possible reactions by the Ten. ·

In most other respects the London Report did not adopt any radical changes.

European Political Cooperation and the EEC[29]

In a sense the original rigid distinction between the Community and the Framework for Political Cooperation was not only counterproductive but also untenable. The persons constituting the leadership of both structures were one and the same, and artificial devices such as separate agendas and even separate meeting places could hardly create a *de facto* separation between the two. Now, not only do the ministers meet in one session, albeit with different agendas, first as the EEC Council of Ministers and then as the Conference of Political Cooperation, but since 1974, in the informal Gymnich-style meetings, the agenda may include both Community and European political cooperation items.

This reality asserted itself also in the Commission's participation in the Framework for Political Cooperation. The 1981 London Report finally affirmed:

> Within the framework of the established rules and procedures the Ten attach importance to the Commission of the European Communities being fully associated with political cooperation, at all levels.

This does not mean that the Commission is a full-fledged participant. It is not privy to the full traffic of COREU nor is it a participant in the group of correspondents. On the other hand it participates, although without decisional power, in meetings of the European Council, the Conference of Foreign Ministers and the Political Committee of Political Cooperation. Any problems of coordination will appear at the operational level, for example within various international organizations where the division of competences between the two groups is not clear, rather than at the central European level.

The most delicate issue however, is not the organizational cooperation and contact between European Community and the Framework for Political Cooperation, but rather the substantive competences of the Community. As we noted above, the resistance of the member states to incorporate political cooperation within the Community is based on two interrelated factors:

> (1) The member states do not wish to submit themselves in matters of foreign policy to the Community's decisional and normative discipline;
> (2) They do not wish the Community, for its part, to expand its competences into fields considered outside the treaties.

But as we have maintained, world affairs do not arrange themselves neatly, respecting the division of competences between Community external relations and European political cooperation. Thus, for example, it is absurd to think that a decision to open trade negotiations with, for example, Yugoslavia or even Israel—matters coming within the exclusive external economic relations competence of the EEC—would not be influenced by political considerations which by current definitions fall under the exclusive jurisdiction of the member states within the Framework for Political Cooperation. The issue may be stated in an even more dramatic form: may decisions on EEC trade and cooperation agreements be formally based on political grounds? This may seem to be an unrealistic and hair-splitting problem, but it has far-reaching constitutional repercussions. In reality, the answer is of course *yes*. But if this *de facto* reply is translated into juridical forms, it would seem that an eventual merger between the Community and the Framework for Political Cooperation is inevitable.

The sensitivity of this issue and its political significance are easily demonstrated in the context of economic sanctions taken by the Community/member states as a political measure. As will be recalled, immediately after the outbreak of the Falklands/Malvina crisis Britain imposed full economic sanctions on Argentina. This in itself was already problematic since economic sanctions, in dry legal language, mean a breach of the Community's Common Commercial Policy. However, the treaty provided in Article 224 for the possibility of a member state who finds itself in war departing from the normal policy, albeit after consultations with other member states.

What then of the position of the other member states who did not find themselves at war with Argentina? It is plausible that in such a situation the language of Article 224 would allow them to join in the sanctions on an individual basis. The Article speaks of:

[M]easures which a member state may be called upon to take in the event . . . of war or serious international tension constituting the threat of war. . . .

Be the legal argument as it may,[30] the member states took another course of action. The Preamble to Council Regulation (EEC) 877/82 of 16 April 1982—a strict Community legal measure—provided, *inter alia*:

The Council of the European Community

Whereas the serious situation resulting from the invasion of the Falkland Islands by Argentina . . . has given rise to discussions in the context of European political cooperation which have led in particular to the decision that economic measures will be taken with regard to Argentina in accordance with the relevant provisions of the Community Treaties; . . .

Whereas . . . it has proved important to take urgent and uniform measures; whereas the member states have therefore decided to adopt a Council Regulation pursuant to the Treaty;

> Whereas . . . the interests of the Community and the member states demand the temporary suspension of imports of all products originating in Argentina; . . .
>
> has adopted this Regulation: . . .
>
> Imports of all products originating in Argentina . . . are hereby suspended.

This remarkable document is interesting for several reasons. First, it clearly illustrates the almost inevitable breakdown on the institutional level of the demarcation between EEC and European Political Cooperation (EPC). Second, it illustrates that if the political will exists, the Ten within the Framework for Political Cooperation have at their disposal more than declarations as instruments of foreign policy. Third, the formal decision imposing sanctions was constituted on the basis of Article 113 of the Treaty of Rome, and was thus to be considered a measure fully within the exclusive Common Commercial Policy of the EEC. Here then was a case in which the member states within the Framework for Political Cooperation "borrowed" a Community instrument to further their political goals. In addition, strict reading would suggest that henceforth the Community decisional process could legitimately resolve to impose economic sanctions, that the decision would be binding on recalcitrant member states and, most dramatically of all, that since the Common Commercial Policy was exclusive, such action could not be taken by the member states outside the Community framework.[31] We have here then in a microcosm both the utility—in terms of efficacy—of a Community foreign-policy action and the danger—in terms of loss of autonomy—to the member states of such a course of action.

Needless to say, the member states reacted to the potential dangers. For example, Denmark, relying on a dubious interpretation of a safeguard measure in the treaty, insisted on implementing the sanctions decision by an act of its own Parliament, reasserting member state sovereignty and underlining the exceptional character of the particular situation.

It is thus inevitable that in the future the artificial gap between the Community and the Framework for Political Cooperation will narrow still further, even if a formal integration of the two is still far away.

Political Cooperation Policy-Making:
Active, Reactive and Reflexive

The mechanisms which we have described above allow the member states to coordinate their positions and, if the political will exists, to adopt a common position and even common action. Given this limited operational range, what may realistically be achieved through the Framework? Let us consider the Framework for Political Cooperation in the context of the classical distinctions, borrowed from the analysis of economic policy, between aims/objectives and instruments/measures.[32] It is here that our earlier allusion to active, reactive and reflexive policy assumes greater significance. It is important to remember that these terms are essentially didactic; in reality one will fuse into the other. But they may help us evaulate the successes and failures of the Framework.

An active policy will seek to influence events directly, to posit "Europe" as an initiator of policy and a veritable world actor. Active policy would typically be predicated on the belief that all events with an international implication are relevant to the actor.

A reactive policy will be one which is less concerned with direct influence, but rather with reacting to world events in order to minimize the costs to the reactive actor.

Under various guises these two elements exist in most interstate foreign policy making.

European political cooperation introduces a third policy component in addition to the active and reactive ones, namely reflexive policy. Here the chief, though rarely exclusive, concern will be the actual formation of a common policy as an integrative value *per se*.

It should be noted, especially in the context of the Middle East conflict, that the transnational nature of the reflexive policy within the Political Cooperation Framework allows for an external dimension as well through the evolution of what has been called the shield effect. Member states may adopt a reactive position, for example critical of Israel, and attribute it to the discipline of the common European policy established within political cooperation. The shield effect could, in principle, operate also on the internal political level: for example a government, faced with internal parliamentary or popular opposition to a course of foreign policy, could justify it as following the common European line. Reflexive policy could be given a less charitable interpretation: it might be regarded as substitute politics—an empty gesture of European make-believe integration which is in reality a cover-up for a failure to deal with the more pressing internal problems of Europe.

The active-reactive-reflexive triangle may relate also to the instruments and measures adopted for the execution of the policy. What instruments are available to the Framework?

In one sense none at all—except the common declaration (at times a potent instrument in international affairs). In another sense, the Framework has at its disposal the entire array of instruments of the member states as well as those belonging to the Community. The tendency to use the declaration as the most common output of the Framework might suggest a paucity of means which conditions a reactive/reflexive orientation. This perception in our view would be a mistake. Given the political will, the member states have at their disposal not only the Community instruments such as retortion or sanction but also every combination of national policy instrument. If the Framework has failed to assert itself actively the reason lies in the lack of political will or substantive agreement among the partners, and not in the absence of instruments.

We insist on the trichotomy—active/reactive/reflexive—because we believe it permits a better evaluation of the successes and failures of the Framework. We can illustrate this at the risk of anticipating some of our subsequent analysis and conclusions. Let us take for example the famous 1980 Venice Declaration—at face value the European entry into active foreign policy-making in the Middle East—in which Europe proposed an alternative to American peacemaking efforts to the chagrin of the United States, or so it seemed. This was to be characterized as the "European initiative."

In active foreign-policy terms—the actual ability to influence events in the region and realize the declared objectives and methods proposed in the Venice Declaration—the European initiative was a failure. In subsequent chapters we shall try to explain the reasons for this failure.

By contrast, in reactive terms (and we return to this theme in our conclusions) the European initiative is at least open to different interpretations. Faced with increasing Arab pressure on European states to take a stronger pro-Arab stand Europe was able to appear to be doing something, while actually not changing her policy substantially. Relations with Israel became strained for a short time, but, there were no economic ramifications. According to this reading of events Europe managed to maintain a precarious relational *status quo*. If we posit a goal of containment rather than one of active influence, we may consider the European initiative less than a failure.

In reflexive terms the Middle East has provided the real laboratory in which all mechanisms of the Framework were tested. And on a declaratory level, the Framework was led to a convergence of European attitudes towards various issues connected with the conflict, such as Palestinian self-determination and a possible role for the PLO. The analytical categories help us thus provide an evaluation of political cooperation output.

Toward a Revised Concept of a European Foreign Policy

How then are we to assess these mechanisms developed for a European foreign policy? The tendency in the literature has often been to dismiss

European foreign policy and especially the Framework for Political Cooperation as a failure, as procedural substitutes for substantive accord, and as entirely reflexive with no active or even reactive element. To the extent that one looks at substantive results we cannot but share these pessimistic conclusions. At the same time, one should not minimize the enormous task which the member states face: they are trying to achieve something which is new and unprecedented in the international arena. The basic premise of the foreign posture is, in the language of the Hague summit:

> [A] Europe composed of States which, while preserving their national characteristics, are united in their essential interests.

The federal state experience, as we already noted, would suggest that the task of preserving national characteristics and statehood while operating a common foreign posture is impossible. And indeed, much of the negative criticism of the Framework for Political Cooperation is typically rooted in a view which has been conditioned by the foreign policy concept developed in other non-unitary entities and especially the federal state. The criticism is usually based on a criterion which adopts an ideal-type model ". . . in which common institutions are in a position to make and carry through all necessary foreign policy decisions for the Community and thereby replace the national foreign policy of the member states."[33]

This ideal-type model is alien not only to the original political cooperation concept which sought to separate the Framework from Community structures. It is also alien to the entire modern trend of European integration in the field of foreign policy which tends to suggest, both in external relations and in political cooperation, a new experiment of a non-unitary foreign policy process and foreign posture which may be called the federal option of foreign affairs.

In order to justify what might appear to be a terminological *faux pas*, two clarifications are necessary. The first concerns the concept of federalism. One often finds in the literature a persistent confusion between, and an erroneous identification of, two distinct concepts: federalism as an organizational principle and a federation (the federal state) as one specific manifestation of that principle. Elazar dispels the confusion by analyzing the etymology of the term which may be found

> first in the biblical hebrew term brit [covenant], then the latin foedus (literally 'covenant') from which the modern "federal" is derived. . . . Elaborated by the Calvinists in their federal theology, the concept formed the basis for far more than a form of political organization. . . . The

original use of the term deals with contractual linkages that involve power sharing—among individuals, among groups, among states. This usage is more appropriate than the definition of modern federations, which represents only one aspect of the federal ideal and one application of the federal principle.[34]

Pescatore reflects the same reasoning in the concrete context of the European Community:

[T]he methods of federalism are not only a means of organizing states. It would rather seem that federalism is a political and legal philosophy which adapts itself to all political contexts on both the municipal and the international level, wherever and whenever two basic prerequisites are fulfilled: the search for unity, combined with genuine respect for the autonomy and the legitimate interests of the participant entities.[35]

As we noted above, the paradox is that federal states typically have a unitary non-federal foreign policy. By contrast it would seem that the Community and its member states, clearly not a federation, are experimenting with a genuine federal foreign policy. In the legal world of external relations the key indicator of this development is found in the growing usage of the so-called mixed agreement, which involves participation in one and the same international treaty of the Community, its member states and the third state. The first agreements between the Community and Israel were of a "pure" Community type; more recent financial and cooperation protocols were of this mixed federal type. In the political world the expression of this federal rationale is the Framework for Political Cooperation, which rejects a unitarist centrist model in favor of the far more complex cooperative model.

How does the federal concept measure up against the objectives of the Framework for Political Cooperation? Compared to the reflexive objectives it might seem that this federal conception is at odds with a vigorous notion of integration or is at least a second-best way of achieving integrational goals. However, we reject this conclusion as too simplistic. It rests on a crude and perhaps outmoded center-periphery model according to which: (1) political systems always have a center and periphery; (2) it is what happens in the center which is politically important; (3) integration consists of constructing a powerful center to which the periphery will be tied. This has not only been the "pontifical" dogma of the Commission and the Court of Justice, but has also been the open or tacit concept in most, though not all, of the literature on the European Community.

The alternative to this view, expressed in modern federal theory,[36] rejects the center-periphery model and regards federalism as a structure which embraces the body politic, rather than one which provides a focus. On this basis integration is no longer measured in terms of center-periphery relationships but rather in the cohesion of the framework as a whole. Integration means a strengthening of whole and parts together and interdependently. Mixed agreement in the legal world and political cooperation in the political world correspond perhaps to this reflexive model. Certainly the member states maintain their power and international profile—but they enhance their capacity to act out of a common position and on occasion even in concert.

Thinking along the lines of a federal concept necessitates as well a reevaluation of the active and reactive objectives and instruments of the system. Perhaps the most sacred cow of political cooperation phraseology has been the oft-repeated slogan that the Framework enabled Europe to speak with one voice. This was to become not merely a mobilizing political instrument but also received an intellectual underpinning by those who asserted that through this unison of voice and action Europe would best be able to actualize in the international field the enormous power consonant with the Ten's importance. Standard critique has been that through Europe's inability to speak with one voice this potential has not in fact been realized.

At the risk of slaughtering this sacred cow, could it be that even on the non-reflexive level there might be advantages to abandoning, at least on occasion, the one voice concept? To be sure, in many situations it will be through concerted and unified action that Europe will best be able to construct an effective policy. At the same time, there may be situations where the united concept will represent a loss—a loss of the potentialities inherent in a pluralistic foreign posture. One voice could represent a loss of subtlety, a need to choose only single options and the risk of dichotomizing reaction to such a single European policy. A pluralistic approach, perhaps more difficult to formulate, would give Europe the potential to play a more subtle "game." For example it might take advantage of the special historical connections of the member states to the objects of the policy. Consider in this context the different relationships which Holland, Denmark, Britain and Germany have towards, and the perception of those states in, Israel. Or the different positions adopted by the member states might put pressure on other actors while keeping communications open.

We do not propose to elaborate on this point much further. If we were to translate it into a slogan we should say that the descriptive and prescriptive trend of European foreign policy is towards a Europe singing like a choir—remembering of course that the choir concept is not meant to replace totally the one voice. Sometimes the choir sings in unison, other times in several voices, and occasionally there are even opportunities for soloists.

Conclusion: European Foreign Policy and the Arab-Israeli Conflict

We are now in a position to consider our central theme—the formulation and execution of European policy towards Israel in the context of the Arab-Israeli conflict. The conflict has been one of the the principal objects of political cooperation statements and delarations. In many ways it offers the best possible prism through which to evaluate the ability of Europe to realize the objectives of a common external posture. It illustrates all three policy components—active, reactive and reflexive—and highlights the mechanisms at their weakest and most ineffective. It also provides us with a laboratory in which to examine the different conceptual frameworks in order to understand European foreign policy making. We shall return to these themes at the conclusion to this book.

TWO

European Political Cooperation and the Arab-Israeli Conflict: 1970–1982

Until the Hague Summit (1–2 December 1969) the six member states of the European Economic Community had done very little in the field of a joint foreign policy.[37]

This could be seen, on the very eve of the Six-Day War, when the Heads of State and Government of the member states met in Rome. During this summit meeting, European leaders only discussed the candidacies of Great Britain, Ireland, Norway and Denmark. In the very midst of a major international crisis, the Six were unable to come to an agreement about principles either of political collaboration or consultation.[38] De Gaulle's suggestion that meetings of foreign ministers be held regularly was rejected by Belgium and, above all, by Dutch Prime Minister De Jongh. Then when the war broke out, each of the Six adopted separate and conflicting positions.

The French condemned Israel, accusing it of being "the first to shoot," and adopted a pro-Arab policy.[39] Germany proclaimed its "neutrality," but in fact strongly supported Israel[40] and called for freedom of navigation in the Gulf of Akaba. Italian governing circles were divided: Animtore Fanfani adopted a rather pro-Arab attitude, while the majority of the Christian Democrats, the Socialists of Pietro Nenni and President Saragat assured Israel of their friendship and understanding.[41] Belgium and Luxemburg tried to find recourse in UN and NATO institutions.[42] The position that Holland adopted was completely opposed to that of France: it fully supported Israeli positions and asserted that the Middle East crisis had been caused by the hostile actions of the Arab states and of the USSR.[43] (However, Holland criticized the annexation of East Jerusalem as soon as it was approved by the Knesset.)

The EEC Commission expressed support for Israel in its own way: on 7 June, in the midst of the war, it approved the conclusions of a report which recommended a status of "associated state" for Israel.

It must be noted that France took a pro-Arab stand, but the *Palestinian* dimension of the conflict was not yet well perceived, not even by De Gaulle. The Palestinean Liberation Organization had been established in 1964 but it was not until 1968 that it was to become an important factor. In 1967, the European states accepted Resolution 242 and none objected to the use of the word "refugees."

During the six years between 1967 and the Yom Kippur War, the problem of the "Arab refugees" was to become the problem of the "legitimate rights of the Palestinians." Only from 1969 onwards did the European Community begin the preparations of a joint foreign policy on the Israeli-Arab conflict.

The Schumann Paper (1971)

After the Hague Summit, which was convened and dominated by the new French president, Georges Pompidou, the political directors of the six foreign ministries prepared the so-called Davignon Report on political cooperation and it was accepted in 1970 by the foreign ministers. The first topic to be chosen—presumably because it was thought to offer the best opportunity to reach a consensus or at least a harmonization of the Six's foreign policies—was the Arab-Israeli conflict. In the eyes of the Israeli government of Golda Meir, this development was an alarming one: it meant that the policies of the EEC members which had been completely divergent at the time of the Six-Day War in three years, had become sufficiently reconciled to achieve some measure of coordination. The Israelis perceived the reflexive element of the EPC as having a potentially negative impact on the supportive policies of its friends among the Six. Reflexivity was considered one-directional: coordination away from Israel.

And indeed since 1969 there had been a slow change of course of several European countries towards the Arab world. Let us take three examples, among the staunchest friends of Israel: Joseph Luns of Holland visited Saudi Arabia and Kuwait in January 1971 and on his return he criticized "all" the parties in the conflict for "not wanting to make concessions."[44] Pierre Harmel of Belgium repeatedly called on Israel to give up all "expansionist" plans, and he toughened Belgium's policy regarding the status of Jerusalem; Aldo Moro's visit to Cairo precipitated a trip by Israeli foreign Minister Abba Eban to make sure, according to the Israeli press, that Italy "was not falling into the Arab camp."

In 1970 it seemed only a matter of a "change of atmosphere," as the differences between the orientations of France's five partners and Pompidou's Middle Eastern policy swept away any chance of a joint statement or even a joint working paper. Thus, at the first political cooperation meeting in Munich in 1970, there was a clash in the positions on the Middle East.[45] In February 1971, dissension again appeared in the midst of the Political Committee, which was entrusted with studying the possibility of publishing a joint paper. Differences of opinion applied just as much to the fate of the refugees as to the demilitarized zones to be set up, the composition of the troops to be stationed there, the question of Jerusalem, etc. The Six had decided that each country would prepare a report on a specific topic: the Dutch presented a report on freedom of navigation, the Italians on the status of Jerusalem. At first this technique failed, because each of the Six advocated its own position in its report and did not try to find a common denominator. Between February and May 1971, France convinced its five partners that there was an urgent need to reach a consensus, at least before the accession of the three new member states to the Common Market. A reconciliation between the six positions was effected and, as feared by Israel, this meant a joint move by the Five toward French foreign policy. In early May everyone knew that the proclamation of a "joint paper" was imminent.

Despite an intensive diplomatic campaign by Israel which warned the EEC against an "unbalanced text"[46] a paper was worked out and unanimously approved by the European foreign ministers on 13 May 1971. Details of the paper were not immediately made public, because the main supporters of Israel (Germany and Holland) apparently insisted that its contents be kept secret. Several points of the report were finally disclosed by the Springer group press in Berlin (*Die Welt*), which mounted a campaign against it.

The main points of this document were:

1. The establishment of demilitarized zones on both sides of Israel-Arab borders.
2. The presence of international forces in these demilitarized zones; the four major powers would *not* be part of these forces.
3. Israel-Arab borders should be those which existed on 4 June 1967.
4. An international status must be given to Jerusalem.
5. Arab refugees must be given the choice between repatriation to their home towns and villages or compensation (according to Article 11 of the 1949 UN resolution).[47]

A remark must be made about the Schumann paper: it was perfectly consistent with UN Resolution 242. The paper refers to "Arab refugees" and not to "Palestinians." Moreover, the Palestinian dimension was merely *one* of the topics dealt with by the Six, whereas later it was to become the crux of the EEC's resolutions or statements. However, given the balance of power within the Community's stand regarding the Palestinian refugee problem, it did damage political relations with Israel.[48] From the Europeans' point of view, their purpose at that stage (before the oil crisis) was not to formulate an active or reactive foreign policy goal but rather to flex their new muscles in the EPC framework. In other words, the goal was more internal than external.

On the other hand, it harmonized quite well with the development of the positions of each of the EEC member states at the beginning of the 1970s. Belgium's Foreign Minister Harmel underlined the importance of the Six's unanimity (and even of the Ten's, because the four candidates to the EEC's membership, which included Norway at the time, had been consulted and had approved the text) when he spoke of the "Printemps de l'Europe."

Only in Germany did the Schumann paper arouse a hostile reaction.[49] Strongly attacked by the press, Walter Schell reacted by asserting that this document was merely a working paper without any practical consequences. On a visit to Israel in July 1971, he even declared that it constituted a simple basis for further discussion between European countries. Such an attempt to minimize the Schumann paper provoked an angry reaction from the French government. However, this affair shows the limits at that time of an EEC common position on the Arab-Israeli conflict.

Until the Yom Kippur War, there had been no other "joint paper" on the Middle East problem. But *each* of the Nine continued to develop a positive reassessment of Arab demands. For each of the Nine the reasons and the rhythm of this evolution were different but the direction was the same. Relations with Israel continued to deteriorate, which is why, not withstanding the war, the time was ripe for the EEC to make a major political move by the end of 1973.[50]

To illustrate these individual trends, we can take the case of West Germany, which was one of the most pro-Israel countries in 1967. By the end of 1972 the German government had freed the three Palestinians who had been arrested at the time of the Munich massacre, and relations with Israel became so strained that the latter recalled its ambassador for consultations. When Willy Brandt visited Israel just before the Yom Kippur War, it became clear that Germany was prepared to give up the "special nature" of its political relations with the Jewish state. Brandt said repeatedly that "Bonn's attitude from now on, would be as objective as possible."[51]

The Joint Declaration of 6 November 1973[52]

During the days which followed the outbreak of the Yom Kippur War, the Nine—just as the Six had done in 1969—adopted divergent positions. On the one hand, the French government persisted in its anti-Israeli stand;[53] on the other hand Holland took an opposite view, holding Egypt and Syria responsible for the hostilities. As for the others, some called for "immediate consultations within the European Community,"[54] and some wanted the Security Council and the UN to intervene. No special meeting was convened by the Nine and they dealt with the events during their "normal" meeting on political cooperation on 11–12 October. Significantly, Holland opposed France and Great Britain "speaking in the name of Europe."[55] All that could be agreed upon, on 13 October, was to issue a rather vague call for a cease-fire and for a solution based on UN Resolution 242.

> Appeal of the Nine Foreign Ministers of 13 October 1973,
> for a Suspension of Hostilities in the Middle East

> The Nine Governments of the European Community, much pre-occupied by the resumption of the fighting in the Middle East, appeal to the parties to agree to stop the hostilities. This cease-fire which would spare the populations affected by the war new and tragic trials, will help at the same time to open the way to a proper negotiation, in an appropriate forum, allowing a solution of the conflict which conforms to all the provisions of Resolution 242 adopted by the Security Council on 22 November 1967 to be put into effect.

The advent of the oil crisis introduced a new currency into European foreign policy. On 20 October, the Arab producers imposed an embargo on Holland, and the supplies of other European countries were no longer guaranteed. On the basis of French proposals, consultations took place to work out a joint position which would, more or less, satisfy the Arab world. The French and British labored to convince their partners that it was absolutely necessary to issue a joint European statement.[56] The debate ended on 6 November with the adoption of a document that was very close to the French government's position.

Declaration of the Nine Foreign Ministers of 6 November 1973, in Brussels on the Situation in the Middle East

The Nine Governments of the European Community have continued their exchange of views on the situation in the Middle East. While emphasizing that the views set out below are only a first contribution on their part to the search for a comprehensive solution to the problem, they have agreed on the following:

1. They strongly urge that the forces of both sides in the Middle East conflict should return immediately to the positions they occupied on 22 October in accordance with Resolution 339 and 340 of the Security Council. They believe that a return to these positions will facilitate a solution to other pressing problems concerning prisoners-of-war and the Egyptian Third Army.

2. They have the firm hope that, following the adoption by the Security Council of Resolution No. 338 of 22 October, negotiations will at last begin for the restoration in the Middle East of a just and lasting peace through the application of Security Council Resolution No. 242 in all of its parts. They declare themselves ready to do all in their power to contribute to that peace. They believe that those negotiations must take place in the framework of the United Nations. They recall that the Charter has entrusted to the Security Council the principal responisibility for international peace and security. The Council and the Secretary-General have a special role to play in the making and keeping of peace through the application of Council Resolutions Nos. 242 and 338.

3. They consider that a peace agreement should be based particularly on the following points:

- the inadmissibility of the acquisition of territory by force;
- the need for Israel to end the territorial occupation which it has maintained since the conflict of 1967;
- respect for the sovereignty, territorial integrity and independence of every State in the area and their right to live in peace within secure and recognized boundaries;
- recognition that in the establishment of a just and lasting peace *account must be taken of the legitimate rights of the Palestinians.*

4. They recall that according to Resolution No. 242 the peace settlement must be the object of international guarantees. They consider that such guarantees must be reinforced, among other means, by the dispatch of peace-keeping forces to the demilitarized zones envisaged in Article 2(c) of Resolution No. 242. They are agreed that such guarantees are of primary importance in settling the overall situation in the Middle East in conformity with Resolution No. 242, to which the Council refers in Resolution No. 338. They reserve the right to make proposals in this connexion. . . .

We will only remark on the four points which indicate a change with regard to the 1971 Schumann paper:

1. For the first time the EEC brought up the rights of the Palestinian refugees *in the terminology* used by the Arab world itself: "the legitimate rights of the Palestinians." Or course, the Nine still did *not* say which role these rights should play in a global settlement, and the call was only to take these rights into consideration, but the word "Palestinians" was the most important element of the statement.
2. The concept of "border adjustments" discussed at the time of the Schumann paper is absent in the 1973 document. The latter rather insists on the inadmissibility of acquisition of territories by force, and the necessity for Israel to put an end to the occupation. (The matter of "secure borders" for Israel does come up in the text, but the link between ending the occupation and secure borders is not at all clear.)
3. The declaration brought up a very sensitive topic that every Israeli government had rejected: that Israeli-Arab negotiations should take place within the framework of the United Nations.
4. Finally, it included the concept of "international guarantees" which inspired very little confidence in Israel.

One could perhaps conclude that in general this joint statement was weaker in its operational details than in the principles it espoused. It appears as if the reactive element was emphasized in order to gain Arab support and with little hope of actually influencing events. And indeed, shortly after the 6 November statement the Arab heads of state, meeting in Algiers, expressed their satisfaction with the declaration.

In Western Europe, reactions were much more critical. Jewish communities of France and Great Britain (respectively 700,000 and 400,000 people) were understandably upset. Several members of parliament demanded explanations from their respective governments (especially in the Netherlands, Germany and Denmark).

Nevertheless, even those governments which had been the most hesitant before 6 November were pleased that the Common Market had finally articulated a joint stand. It should not be forgotten that the countries which were still rather pro-Israeli were at the same time the strongest supporters of European political union. The statement was the first joint declaration on an acute foreign policy issue and the first concrete result of the "political cooperation" process. None of the EEC members, even under strong criticism by various influencial pressure groups, intended to give up on this achievement.

The 6 November statement illustrated another internal dimension of the EPC—the ability to shift the forum of foreign policy-making from the national capitals, and thus avoid possible internal restraints, and more important, the use of the reflexive element (European unity etc.) as a justification for a posture which might not have been possible for a government to adopt independently at home.

The Israeli government's reaction was very sharp.[57] In a communiqué on 9 November Foreign Minister Eban pointed out that this statement meant "Oil for Europe" and not "Peace in the Middle East." He said that the declaration revealed "feudal considerations, which allowed very little room for sovereignty of the States concerned." The document "was issued at an extremely unfortunate moment" and "was ill-timed." Eban added that the only aim of the Nine was to try to persuade the Arab governments not to cut down on their oil exports to Europe. The statement contained a formulation of the territorial problem "devoid of any international legal basis," and it "did not bind Israel in any way whatsoever," because it "did not take into account the opinion of the states which are the most concerned." Eban spoke against the "principles which had prompted the drawing up of the text," a text which underlined "imperatively" the manner in which Israeli-Arab negotiations "should" take place, how peace "should" be guaranteed, and what "should" be done for the Palestinians. In conclusion, the European Community behaved as if Israel and its neighbors were not sovereign states and "were still living in the ancient bonds of servitude." "The least the world could do, if it wants to contribute to a sovereign and negotiated peace," said Eban, "is precisely to refrain from making such declarations in the future."[58]

The Eban rejection set the tone for subsequent Israeli reactions to European intervention. The governments of Golda Meir, Yitzhak Rabin, Menahem Begin and Yizhak Shamir all in turn objected to European declarations, papers, and statements; the EEC could legitimately help the parties, the sovereign states of the Middle East, to meet one another, to hold direct negotiations, but in no way could it "dictate" the principles of a peace settlement. In some ways, the Israelis agreed to the Community's assumption of the purely technical role that France played during the Paris negotiations between the United States and Vietnam; i.e., to settle material problems, to create a good atmosphere, to offer its services, but *not* to interfere with the terms of a peace settlement. Indeed, after the "bias" revealed by the 6 November statement the Israeli view was to limit the European political intervention to a minimum.

Implementing the November 1973 Declaration

In the ensuing period (1973–1977), the Nine tried to enhance this reactive policy and even build some active elements into it. Thus, at the December 1973 Copenhagen Summit, the Heads of State and Government reaffirmed their wish to please the Arab world.

The Copenhagen Statement

1. The nine countries affirmed their common will that Europe should speak with one voice in important world affairs. . . .
2. They decided to speed up the work required to define the European Union which they had set themselves as their major objective at the Paris Summit. They asked the President to make the necessary proposals without delay.
3. They decided to meet more frequently. These meetings will be held whenever justified by the circumstances and when it appears necessary to provide a stimulus or to lay down further guidelines for the construction of a united Europe. They also agreed to meet whenever the international situation so requires. . . . The Heads of State and Government attach the greatest importance to the institutions of the community playing their full role and to the necessary decisions being taken there in good time.
4. It was agreed that the Foreign Ministers of the member states should, at their next meeting, decide on the means by which a common position should be worked out quickly in times of crisis. The development of political cooperation will also enable them to make joint assessments of crisis situations, with the aim of foreseeing them and of taking the measures needed to deal with them. . . .
5. The Heads of State and Government welcome the convening of a peace conference in Geneva and call on the participants to make every effort to achieve a just and lasting settlement at an early date. The Nine governments are ready to assist in the search for peace and in the guaranteeing of a settlement.
6. The Heads of State and Government reaffirmed the united stand of their governments on the Middle East question embodied in the Declaration issued on 6 November. Recent events have strengthened them in their view that the security of all states in the area, whether it be Israel or her Arab neighbors, can only be based on the full implementation of Security Council Resolution 242 in all its parts taking into account also the legitimate rights of the Palestinians.
7. The Heads of State and Government are convinced that the requirements of sovereignty and the requirements of security can be met by the conclusion of peace agreements including among

other arrangements international guarantees and the establishment of demilitarized zones.

An analysis of the votes of the nine European states during the 28th session of the General Assembly (1973) shows that[59] the Nine voted *for* the resolutions criticizing Israel in line with the terms (or the spirit) of their joint statement of 6 November, and voted *against* those Arab, Communist or Third-World resolutions which recognized Palestinan right to self-determination or condemned Israel in terms which were beyond the limits of their joint statement. The Nine abstained when a question arose which would sharply divide them, for example when the rights of the Palestinians were called "inalienable" or when the Jewish settlements were discussed. Following their informal meeting with four Arab ministers at the end of the Copenhagen Summit, the European leaders attempted to initiate a Euro-Arab dialogue.[60] From the EEC's perspective, the dialogue's aim was to secure European oil imports while making a major effort to help Arab economic development. The objective was to promote extensive Euro-Arab cooperation in every economic field: the Europeans would invest large sums in Arab industrial, as well as agricultural, development, while the Arabs would promise to furnish their oil without any interruption and at reasonable prices. The dialogue was the main topic of various European-Arab meetings during the spring of 1974 and was officially opened in July 1974 in Paris. Very quickly the Europeans, who had thought, rather naively, that they could conduct this consultation on a strictly economic basis, were confronted with increasing political problems. On the one hand, the US government, especially Secretary of State Kissinger, reacted very sharply to what it saw as a breach in the Occidental front against Arab oil exporters. Washington exerted strong pressures on its closest allies (Britain, Germany, Holland, Italy) to abandon their attempt to deal directly with the Arab world. On the other hand, the Arab countries, even when they did not completely neglect the economic aspects of the dialogue, wanted it to be centered on political cooperation, (i.e. the Palestinian question). In short, the Arabs wanted to politicize the dialogue and to use it as an instrument in their war against Israel. For example, from the beginning, the Arabs requested from the EEC two major concessions: (1) to give up the free-trade agreement which was to be signed with Israel in 1975; (2) to allow an independent representation of the PLO in the dialogue's general commission and the expert committees.

Europe took a firm stand against these two demands. They would have meant a major change in the EEC's policy toward Israel and the PLO, and the majority of the Nine were *not* prepared in 1974–75 to make such a move. The free-trade agreement with Israel was signed in

May 1975,[61] and the Nine vigorously objected to independent PLO representation in the dialogue. Ultimately a compromise was achieved by establishing only two delegations: one European and the other Arab. In the latter, the Arab countries could include, if they wished, a Palestinian representative.

Even as the Europeans stood firm, they were confronted with repeated Arab attempts to have them recognize the PLO, recognize the right of the Palestinians to self-determination and statehood, and to condemn Israel more strongly. The Arabs used the dialogue to induce the Europeans to change their 1973 statement and go a step further. In Cairo, (June 1975), Rome (July 1975), Abu-Dhabi (November 1975), Luxemburg (May 1976) and especially Tunis (February 1977), the Arabs posited a new European stand on the Palestinian problem as a condition of any success in the "ecomomic" dialogue. At the Tunis meeting, the Arab countries warned the Europeans that if they did not issue a new statement on the Middle East the dialogue would be seriously jeopardized. For the first time at Tunis, the Nine agreed to discuss "political" issues with the Arab League, and this signalled a success for the latter. In 1973–1977, the bilateral relations between each of the Nine and Israel deteriorated. Each European state reached the conclusion that some meaning should be given to the 1973 concept of Palestinian "legitimate rights."

The main topic of the 29th session of the UN General Assembly (autumn 1974) was the Palestinian problem. While France, Ireland and Italy voted in favor of the resolution inviting the PLO to participate in the Assembly debates; and when the Eight voted against Resolution 3237 granting the PLO permanent observer status, France abstained. No doubt the relations between the European countries and Israel were becoming increasingly strained, due in part to the PLO's 1974 diplomatic offensive.

Relations between West Germany and Israel also became tense after Chancellor Brandt visited Algeria and Egypt in April 1974, with the official purpose of promoting Euro-Arab cooperation. Bonn issued more and more statements which insisted on Israeli withdrawal from *all* the territories and on the rights of the Palestinian people.

Even Israel's three staunchest allies in the EEC, Holland, Denmark and Luxemburg, slowly began to change and follow the same direction. Criticism of Jewish settlements in the territories became vehement. The mass media of these countries—for whom the term "PLO" had once been taboo—brought up the Palestinian issues with ever-increasing insistence. Public opinion in Israel was angered by the Netherlands government's refusal to allow Princess Beatrix and Prince Claus to enter East Jerusalem in 1976.

These bilateral developments involved all EEC countries albeit in different degrees.

Without any connection to the Middle East, there was an intensification of the political cooperation process among the Nine. An important decision was reached at the Paris Summit in December 1974. The Heads of State and Government resolved to meet henceforth three times a year as a "European Council" and to intensify their consultations in foreign policy in order to formulate common positions. In January of 1977 French President Giscard d'Estaing sent a "letter" to his partners outlining his view on the role of the Council. In this letter he emphasized that the Council was "to make solemn statements in order to make the voice of Europe heard." Giscard's proposals were accepted at the European Council's meeting in London in June 1977. It was very clear that such "joint statements" would be centered, albeit not exclusively, on the Middle East conflict.

Therefore, the London European Council's adopting of a new declaration on the Israeli-Arab conflict was a natural conclusion of the three developments: (1) the feeling that the Euro-Arab dialogue would not go ahead without a new European statement on the Palestinians; (2) the deterioration of bilateral relations between the Nine and Israel; (3) the desire of the Europeans to expand and intensify their "political cooperation" process in the quest for political unity.

The London Statement and the Nine's Reaction to President Sadat's Initiative and to the Peace Treaty

1977 was a crucial year in the context of the political situation in the Middle East and the development of the Arab-Israeli conflict. First, the Likud under the the leadership of Menahem Begin won the legislative elections in Israel.[62] The new leader's rise to power undoubtedly affected relations between Western Europe and Israel. The Israeli prime minister, whose primary interests were foreign and defense policies, had a heavily charged "European past." It should be recalled that he had personally led a violent campaign against the establishment of "normal" relations with Germany in the 1950s and the 1960s. Once in power, his personal distaste for Germany—and for Chancellor Helmut Schmidt—continued to rankle unabated. As for Britain, it is well known that most British statesmen distrusted someone they viewed as a "former terrorist," who had been responsible for blowing up the British headquarters in Jerusalem. When he was elected, Begin did nothing to alleviate this uneasiness. From 1977 he spared no occasion to remind the Europeans of their responsibility for the Holocaust during World War II. These accusations were reinforced by the publications of anti-Israeli European statements. In short, Begin had a "European past" which made him much more difficult to deal with than a Levi Eshkol, a Golda Meir, or a Yitzhak Rabin.

However, beyond the personal dimension, Begin's change of policy regarding the West Bank and the Gaza Strip played a major role in hardening Europe's attitude towards Israel. His was a tougher line, laying claim to all the territories of historic *Eretz Israel* and supporting the increase in Jewish settlements even in parts of the territories heavily populated by Arabs. It would, however, be wrong to present this policy as fundamentally different from the policy of Labor governments before him, all of whom had allowed the development of Jewish settlements, though only in certain areas. It would also be incorrect to assert that it was the policy of the Begin government that caused European-Israeli relations to deteriorate. The change in the Nine's attitudes towards Israel began before Begin came to power and his election only accelerated the process: it constituted a pretext for European governments to stiffen their positions on the conflict. In particular, socialist governments in Western Europe had no more reason to relent in their accusations against Israel, for they were no longer dealing with the Labor party.

Besides the new Israeli policy, the most striking event in 1977 was Egyptian President Sadat's initiative. In November 1977 he visited Jerusalem and this trip paved the way, the following year, for the Camp David agreements and then, in March 1979, for the peace treaty between Israel and Egypt. This unexpected chain of events presented a problem for the EEC, which had to react to each event in turn.

At the June 1977 European Council meeting in London (held exactly one month after the Israeli elections) the Nine endorsed a new joint statement, the most important element of which was the content the Europeans gave to what they had called in 1973 the "legitimate rights" of the Palestinians. In 1977 the EEC stated that expression should be given to these rights through a Palestinian *homeland*.[63] The London declaration also shed new light on other points. By stating that the only solution to the conflict was to recognize the right to a homeland, the Nine placed the Palestinian problem at the very core of the conflict; granting Israel secure borders was no longer *the* essential feature of a peace settlement. The Europeans also urged that representatives of the Palestinian people take part in the negotiations. This could mean local leaders from the territories who were independent, pro-PLO or pro-Jordanian, but it was already clear that the population of the territories identified increasingly with the PLO leadership.

The London Statement (30 June 1977)

1. At the present critical stage in the Middle East, the Nine welcome all efforts now being made to bring to an end the tragic conflict there. They emphasize the crucial interest which they see in early and successful negotiations towards a just and lasting peace. They call on all the parties concerned to agree urgently to participate in such negotiations in a constructive and realistic spirit; at this juncture in particular all parties should refrain from statements or policies which could constitute an obstacle to the pursuit of peace.

2. The Nine set out on many occasions in the past, for example, in their statements of 6 November 1973, 28 September 1976 and 7 December 1976, their view that a peace settlement should be based on Security Council Resolutions 242 and 338 and on:

- the inadmissibility of the acquisition of territory by force;
- the need for Israel to end the territorial occupation which it has maintained since the conflict of 1967;
- respect for the sovereignty, territorial integrity and independence of every state in the area and their right to live in peace within secure and recognised boundaries;
- recognition that in the establishment of a just and lasting peace account must be taken of the legitimate rights of the Palestinians.

It remains their firm view that all these aspects must be taken as a whole.

3. The Nine have affirmed their belief that a solution to the conflict in the Middle East will be possible *only if the legitimate right of the Palestinian people to give effective expression to its national identity is translated into fact, which would take into account the need for a homeland for the Palestinian people.* They consider that the representatives of the parties to the conflict, *including the Palestinian people, must participate in the negotiations* in an appropriate manner to be worked out in consultation between all the parties concerned. In the context of an overall settlement, Israel must be ready to recognise the legitimate rights of the Palestinian people: equally, the Arab side must be ready to recognize the right of Israel to live in peace within secure and recognized boundaries. It is not through the acquisition of territory by force that the security of the states of the region can be assured; but it must be based on commitments to peace exchanged between all the parties concerned with a view to establishing truly peaceful relations. (Emphasis added.)

4. The Nine believe that the peace negotiations must be resumed urgently, with the aim of agreeing and implementing a comprehensive, just and lasting settlement of the conflict. They remain ready to contribute to the extent the parties wish in finding a settlement and in putting it into effect. They are also ready to consider participation in guarantees in the framework of the United Nations.

The London statement supported a position contrary to that of Israel in every respect (whichever Israeli government was in power). The Israelis knew perfectly well what the term *homeland* meant, because the very same term (*ba'it leumi* in Hebrew) was used by the Zionist movement at the time of the British mandate, with the expectation that the homeland would become a sovereign state. Even if the Europeans did not necessarily think of the homeland as the precursor of a sovereign state, that was precisely what it meant for an Israeli. The position of all Israeli governments whether Likud or Maarakh was that the creation of a Palestinian state situated between Israel and Jordan must be rejected. This position was shared across the board by the whole political spectrum in Israel, with the exception of the two extreme left parties, which were marginal: the Communist Party Rakah and Sheli (extreme left Zionists). Moreover, most Israelis viewed with dismay the attempt to focus on the Palestinian problem as the crux of the conflict, since for them the Arab world's refusal to recognize Israel was the central problem. And most Israelis rejected the proposal that Palestinian delegates participate in a peace settlement *on an equal footing* with representatives of sovereign states.

The Israeli reaction to the London declaration was therefore sharply critical, while the Arab states and the PLO, although they considered it insufficient, perceived the declaration as a positive development.

Furthermore, the London statement was totally ill-suited to the events that were to occur in the following months: President Sadat's initiative, the Camp David agreements, and the Israeli-Egyptian peace treaty. In no way could it be used as an "instrument" which would allow the EEC to evaluate and react efficiently to these unexpected events. Why?

1. The European text carried weight only as long as the Community was one of the major factors in the Middle East. After Camp David the United States became the only decisive (Occidental) factor in the area, and this pushed Western Europe completely into the background. The close ties certain EEC members had with the US posed quite a problem for these countries as the US government asked them explicitly not to interfere in Middle East affairs.

2. The context of the London statement was one in which no Arab country had recognized Israel or was ready to talk with her. Not only had Egypt, the most important Arab country, recognized the Jewish state, but it also had started negotiating with her about a solution to the Palestinian problem.

3. The solution that Israel and—in theory—Egypt had in mind for the Palestinian problem had, at least overtly, nothing to do with the concept of a homeland, which does not appear in any of the documents connected with the Camp David process; the central concept of the Israeli-Egyptian negotiations was autonomy for the Palestinians living

in the West Bank and the Gaza strip at least for five years. Thus the content of the European initiative, which took shape in 1977, constituted an antithesis of the elements of the major peace process that had involved the Middle East since the creation of Israel. Europe would be in a position to pursue its own course on the Palestinian question only in 1980, when the Camp David process would prove to be a failure in this area.

However, in 1977–1980 the Nine tried to follow the London declaration as much as possible and to react to the events in the Middle East accordingly. The need for a Palestinian homeland was repeated at various times, for example, by Belgian Foreign Minister Henri Simonet (then president of the EEC Council of Ministers) at the 32nd session of the UN General Assembly and at the third session of the Euro-Arab dialogue in Brussels.

At the UN the Nine voted unanimously for those texts which condemned the Israeli occupation and the methods used by Israel in Jerusalem and in the territories. All abstained when the proposed resolutions went far beyond their London declaration. (Before June 1977 certain European countries such as Germany or Holland would have voted against these resolutions.) The French governments of Giscard d'Estaing was still at the fore of the pro-Arab trend, and was the only EEC member to abstain on the resolution which called for a special department for Palestinian rights in the UN Secretariat.

At the 33rd session of the General Assembly at the end of 1978, the Nine stepped up their criticism of Israeli policies. The UN resolution condemning Jewish settlements included terms which were much more severe than before; nevertheless, the Nine endorsed it. The resolution requesting the Secretary General to issue a report *in collaboration with the PLO* on the "occupation" was a completely new element; however, the Nine abstained, with none voting against it. And above all, after Camp David and just when Israel and Egypt were engaged in full-scale negotiations, the Nine abstained on the anti-Camp David resolution calling for the Geneva Conference to be held with the participation of the PLO.[64]

At the 34th session of the General Assembly in 1979, the Nine interpreted their London statement in a markedly more aggressive manner, and signalled their intention to go much further. They did not deviate from their former positions, but one could feel that the groundwork was being laid for a new stage, in which the Community would explicitly bring up the name and the role of the PLO. The following three examples will illustrate the point:

- In 1978 Italy and Luxemburg had voted against the resolution approving the report of the UN Committee for Palestinian Rights; this time they joined France, Ireland and Belgium in abstaining.
- Ireland and Italy voted this time with France for the resolution demanding the participation of the PLO in a future peace conference.
- Michael O'Kennedy, the Irish Foreign Minister, speaking in the General Assembly on behalf of the European Community, for the first time brought up, albeit indirectly, the name of the PLO: O'Kennedy referred to the necessity of all parties concerned in the conflict "including the Palestinian Liberation Organization" to use certain Security Council resolutions along with certain other principles as "an essential framework for a peace settlement."

This short survey of the Europeans' attitude at the UN in 1977–1979 clearly shows a growing insistence on the rights of the Palestinians, and increasing criticism of Israel, and the implied acceptance of the role that the PLO could play, as well as increasing skepticism about the Camp David peace process.

Immediately after Sadat's trip to Jerusalem, France indicated its reservation that what seemed to inaugurate a "separate peace" could not solve the Palestinian problem. On the other hand, its eight partners, although in varying degrees, viewed the Egyptian initiative very favorably. In any case, they did not want to jeopardize this opportunity, which was the first on the road to peace in the Middle East. At the same time, they did not want to impair their rather good relations with the Arab world, of which the Euro-Arab dialogue was an example. And they had to take into account the fact that almost all Arab countries, except Sudan and Oman, condemned Sadat's initiative.

After an initial period of silence, the nine member states issued their 22 November communiqué, expressing their support for "President Sadat's bold initiative" and "the unprecedented dialogue begun in Jerusalem." But they also emphasized the need for "comprehensive negotiations leading to a just and lasting overall settlement," a settlement which would bring peace to the Palestinian people. Above all, they emphasized that the principles governing such a settlement should be those of their London statement (including the need for a homeland for the Palestinians)[65] and insisted on the need to convene the Geneva Conference as soon as possible. This short communiqué was rather lukewarm and very cautious. According to a commentator, "Had it not been for American pressure to make a statement supporting Sadat, the Nine would almost certainly have adopted the 'wait and see' posture urged by the French."[66] The Nine made no new statement until ten months later, despite repeated calls by the Egyptians asking Europe to support the ongoing process. Indeed, the EEC members became increasingly cautious. It appeared that the peace towards which Israel and Egypt were steering was not going to be an "overall settlement"; rather, it was going to be an "American peace" which would not be made under the auspices of the UN nor in the framework of the Geneva Conference.

This feeling of distrust (especially towards Israel) was expressed, for example, in the remarks of Henri Simonet when he came back from the Middle East in March 1978 and the remarks of Danish Prime Minister Joergensen at the end of the European Council of April 1978.

However, the success of Camp David allowed those members of the European Community who were still supporters of an Israeli-Egyptian peace agreement to "get their revenge" and have a favorable European statement adopted. The EEC 19 September 1978 declaration termed Camp David "a further major step towards an (overall) settlement" and the Europeans promised "their strong support to achieve it."[67] This support for Camp David was clearly reiterated at the UN General Assembly's session, a few days later.

Two points should be made:

- On the one hand, this positive attitude of the Nine towards American-Israeli-Egyptian efforts was not to last. As early as the Damascus session of the Euro-Arab dialogue (November–December 1978) the Arab countries, and in particular Syria, demanded that the Community end any support for Camp David and that it recognize the PLO as the only legitimate representative of the Palestinian people. The Nine did not agree to these demands, but they yielded somewhat: they did not insist on their support for Camp David and they agreed that the session's final communiqué should speak of the Palestinian problem as the "central problem" of the Middle East conflict. Thus, they tried to make concessions in order to satisfy the Arabs. Within the Community, France worked very hard to soften the support for Camp David and to yield to the Arab demands.
- On the other hand, even though they became increasingly disillusioned with the results of Camp David, and despite their attempt to start their own "peace initiative" after 1980, the Nine never retracted their positive assessment of the Camp David agreement. We shall see that the Venice Declaration (1980) and post-Venice European efforts were offered as a complement to Camp David rather than an alternative to it.

Immediately after the Israeli-Egyptian peace treaty was concluded, the Community issued a rather cold communiqué (26 March 1979).[68] According to the statement:

> The Nine express the hope that all parties concerned will avoid any statement or action which will impede the search for peace, such as the Israeli policy of settlements in the occupied territories. . . . While a difficult road remains before the implementation of United Nations Resolution 242 on all fronts, the Nine consider that the peace treaty (between Israel and Egypt) constitutes a correct application of the principles of that resolution.

The statement, issued in Paris, said that the EEC countries hoped that the "will for peace" which had led President Carter of the United States to

> engage himself personally in negotiations can be given practical form soon in a comprehensive agreement in which all the parties, including representatives of the Palestinian people, would participate and to which the international community could give its endorsement.
>
> They recall that as they said in their declaration of 29 June 1977, the establishment of a just place in the framework of a comprehensive settlement. Such a settlement must be based on UN resolutions 242 and 338.

And finally:

> In this context they take due note of the will of the signatories to consider this [treaty] as a first step in the direction of a comprehensive settlement designed to end thirty years of hostility.

The lack of enthusiasm for the peace treaty reflected three main factors. First, Arab countries warned that they would consider any West European support for the Israeli-Egyptian peace treaty as a challenge. In the Syrian Foreign Minister's words: "It would not be in Europe's interests to challenge the Arabs. The Europeans should leave such an ungrateful task to the Americans. . . ." In fact, the Eight aligned themselves more or less with the French, who viewed the treaty unfavorably. As soon as the contents of this document were publicized Giscard d'Estaing insisted that only a global settlement could bring about a just and lasting peace in the Middle East. Finally, this lack of enthusiasm reflected the increased tendency of the Europeans to dissociate themselves from President Carter's foreign policy and generally from American options.

The declaration which the Nine issued on 18 June 1979 demonstrated how quickly the Europeans dissociated themselves from the peace treaty.[69]

This statement completely ignored the treaty and did not intimate any approval for the Israeli and Egyptian diplomatic efforts. Instead, it insisted on the 1977 London Declaration and the need for a homeland, called Israel's policy in the occupied territories a stumbling block in the way of a global peace settlement, declared Jewish settlements illegal, and sharply condemned (Israeli) attacks on South Lebanon.

After this declaration, during the autumn of 1979 and the spring of 1980, all the members of the European Community slowly reached a consensus that some kind of partial and unofficial recognition should be given to the PLO. There were several reasons for such a development. First, the Nine were convinced that the negotiations between Israel and Egypt on autonomy would lead to a deadlock; second, the question of the rights of the Palestinians had definitely taken precedence over any other consideration in the ruling European parties; third, the Nine wanted to encourage the "moderate" Arab countries to join the peace process and they knew that recognition of the PLO was the price to pay. Finally, the Europeans felt that *they* had to launch a concrete Middle East peace initiative and that even if the latter sought to complement Camp David, it should nevertheless insert *new* components in order to please the Arab world. The Arab countries, through France and England, placed increasing pressure on the European Community to play a more active role, and they insisted that the EEC present its own proposals for a peace settlement, proposals which should be very distinctly separate from American efforts.

On the other hand, the very harsh tone of Foreign Minister Dayan's speech in Strasbourg in October 1979 showed that the Israeli government had decided to quash any European initiative which would be based on a recognition of the PLO or which would deviate from Camp David.

The Venice Declaration and the Development of the "European Initiative" Until the 1982 Lebanon War

The Elaboration of the Venice Declaration and Israeli Efforts Aimed at Preventing It

As early as February 1980, Lord Carrington declared that, as the Camp David process had come to a halt, a European initiative had become necessary. The French president, after his trip to the Gulf States where he proclaimed the Palestinians' right to "self-determination,"[70] tried to persuade his partners to adopt a similar position. Some time later, Foreign Minister Henri Simonet told the Belgian Parliament that the French position was in fact held by all nine states. Concurrently, a senior Dutch foreign ministry official, Naboth Van Dijl, held talks with Abdel Hassan Abu Maizer, a member of the PLO's Executive Committee, as part of a deliberate effort by the Netherlands to improve contacts with the PLO.

Point 4 of the Declaration of the European Council (29 April 1980 at Luxemburg) indicated that at the next meeting in Venice the foreign ministers were to present a report on how Europe could contribute to peace in the Middle East, because "Europe may in due course have a role to play."

The European initiative, planned for the spring of 1980 could have taken a number of forms. Some observers thought that the "initiative" would be a collective attempt to have UN Resolution 242 modified, by replacing the word "refugees" with the word "Palestinians." On the other hand, the Community could assert the right of the Palestinians to "self-determination," and recognize the PLO as *the* representative of the Palestinians in future negotiations. Another possibility was that by keeping a "low profile" Europe could simply propose a new way to get the autonomy negotiations out of their deadlock. In short, all the options seemed open.

The atmosphere was favorable for a European initiative: the question of the British contribution to the European budget had been settled,[71] the Afghanistan affair had induced everyone to take action to counteract the Soviet Union's influence in every way possible, and the whole world seemed convinced that the negotiations on Palestinian autonomy had definitely reached an impasse.

The Americans and the Israelis did all they could to prevent the Europeans from issuing a new statement which could begin a process divergent from Camp David. The Carter administration brought all its weight to bear on those EEC countries which were the most closely bound to the US. The "European initiative" was depicted as an act of open hostility towards America. Carter was especially anxious to prevent European action because he was seeking re-election and Camp David was his main asset. Carter asserted that the US would not hestitate to use its veto power to prevent any modification of UN Resolution 242 and asked the Europeans to wait, and "not to commit themselves for the time being in the Palestinian autonomy question."[72] In order to prevent such a European initiative, the Americans (and the Israelis) kept repeating that the tripartite autonomy talks were to begin very shortly.

The US mitigated its pressure at the beginning of June 1980 after Emilio Colombo, then President of the EEC Council, explained to Secretary of State Edmund Muskie that the Europeans *did not* want to oppose Camp David, and that they only wished to be "constructive."[73]

It is probable that the American pressure succeeded in making the Venice Declaration much more "moderate" than had been previously expected.

In the meantime Israel embarked on one of the biggest diplomatic offensives of its history. All Israeli political parties (except the extreme left) expressed total opposition to what was predicted to be the content of the next European statement.

Menahem Begin, speaking at the Knesset on 2 June 1980, announced that any European initiative based on the rights of the Palestinians to "self-determination" would immediately be rejected by Israel.[74] He sent a copy of the PLO Charter to all European Heads of State and Government. Foreign Minister Shamir went on a tour of European capitals on the eve of the European Council meeting to convince EEC members that the new statement they were about to issue would be particularly inopportune. It seems that at least two of those with whom he spoke (the Netherlands' and Luxemburg's foreign ministers) promised him that there would *not* be a real European initiative.[75]

The Labor opposition, with Abba Eban as its spokesman, also opposed any European intervention. (This is important, given that in the summer of 1980 everyone predicted an extraordinary victory for the Labor Party in the Knesset elections to be held the following year.) In a leading article which appeared in the *London Times* of 13 June, Eban explained why all the parties in Israel rejected a European initiative:

> The answer lies, first of all, in West Europe's failure of self-criticism. In a region where we have learned to be grateful for small mercies, the past seven years have seen large results for concilation. . . . But in all this work of concilation, the contribution of the EEC and its present governments was zero. . . . Europe of course, had a sovereign right to fix its own priorities and to put its oil supplies at the head of the list. But having placed a parochial and mercantile approach above Israel's survival and western solidarity, Europe could not expect to be taken seriously as a disinterested conciliator. . . . The shower of European statements in favour of Palestinian "self-determination" was recently inaugurated by President Giscard d'Estaing in Kuwait. Now Kuwait is not the natural arena for proclaiming the rights of man. . . . A European pretence of total altruism is sanctimonious and unconvincing.

Then Abba Eban pointed out "some of the errors that contributed to Europe's exclusion hitherto" as a viable partner.

> Its primary fallacy has been to underestimate the importance of the Egyptian-Israeli treaty.

It is legitimate for Europe to hope for a change in the Palestinian attitude towards Israel's sovereignty and safety. But you do not produce a change by pretending that it has happened when it has not even begun to occur;

Another European fallacy consists of a strange disregard for Western solidarity. . . . Europe can play a role only in a context of Western harmony;

There is a European tendency to isolate the Palestine issue from its Jordanian context;

Another European error is to overestimate the value of semantic gimmicks. Self-determination, like most international slogans, is neutral and ambivalent. . . . Nothing could be more irresponsible than to assert self-determination as an absolute and exclusive Palestinian right without regard to its consequences for Israel's security and Middle Eastern peace.

The whole of the Israeli press and public opinion became enraged at the possibility of a European intervention. On the eve of the Venice meeting, the Belgian paper *Le Soir* wrote: "We should be aware that the great majority of the Israel nation, the young and the old, the ultra and the moderate, the new immigrants and the Sabras have a very poor image of Europe."[76] Israeli papers noted that the Europeans were moving closer to the PLO, only a few days after the Damascus meeting of this organization on 31 May at which *Al-Fatah* leaders said: "The Fatah has pledged to continue its struggle until the total destruction of the Zionist entity, from every point of view: economic, political, cultural, military and ideological."

The Venice Declaration and the Reaction of the Parties

On 13 June 1980, the Heads of State and Government of the Nine, meeting at the European Council in Venice, adopted a fundamental resolution on the Middle East.[77]

The Venice Declaration

1. The Heads of State and Government and the Ministers of Foreign Affairs held a comprehensive exchange of views on all aspects of the present situation in the Middle East, including the state of negotiations resulting from the agreements signed between Egypt and Israel in March 1979. They agreed that growing tensions affecting this region constitute a serious danger and render a comprehensive solution to the Israeli-Arab conflict more necessary and pressing than ever.
2. The nine member states of the European Community consider that the traditional ties and common interests which link Europe to the Middle

East oblige them to play a special role and now require them to work in a more concrete way towards peace.

3. In this regard, the nine countries of the Community base themselves on Security Council Resolutions 242 and 338 and the positions which they have expressed on several occasions, notably on their Declaration of 29 June 1977, 19 September 1978, 26 March and 18 June 1979, as well as in the speech made on their behalf on 25 September 1979 by the Irish Minister of Foreign Affairs at the 34th United Nations General Assembly.

4. On the bases thus set out, the time has come to promote the recognition and implementation of the two principles universally accepted by the international community: the rights to existence and to security of all the states in the region, including Israel, and justice for all the peoples, which implies the recognition of the legitimate rights of the Palestinian people.

5. All of the countries in the area are entitled to live in peace within secure, recognized and guaranteed borders. The necessary guarantees for a peace settlement should be provided by the UN by a decision of the Security Council and, if necessary, on the basis of other mutually agreed procedures. The Nine declare that they are prepared to participate within the framework of a comprehensive settlement in a system of concrete and binding international guarantees, including (guarantees) on the ground.

6. A just solution must finally be found to the Palestinian problem, which is not simply one of refugees. The Palestinian people, which is conscious of existing as such, must be placed in a position, by an appropriate process defined within the framework of the comprehensive peace settlement, to exercise fully its right to self-determination.

7. The achievement of these objectives requires the involvement and support of all the parties concerned in the peace settlement which the Nine are endeavoring to promote in keeping with the principles formulated in the declaration referred to above. These principles apply to all the parties concerned, and thus the Palestinian people, and to the PLO, which will have to be associated with the negotiations.

8. The Nine recognize the special importance of the role played by the question of Jerusalem for all the parties concerned. The Nine stress that they will not accept any unilateral initiative designed to change the status of Jerusalem and that any agreement on the city's status should guarantee freedom of access for everyone to the Holy Places.

9. The Nine stress the need for Israel to put an end to the territorial occupation which it has maintained since the conflict of 1967, as it has done for part of Sinai. They are deeply convinced that the Israeli settlements constitute a serious obstacle to the peace process in the Middle East. The Nine consider that these settlements, as well as modifications in population and property in the occupied Arab territories, are illegal under international law.

10. Concerned as they are to put an end to violence, the Nine consider that only the renunciation of force or the threatened use of force by all the

parties can create a climate of confidence in the area, and constitute a basic element for a comprehensive settlement of the conflict in the Middle East.

11. The Nine have decided to make the necessary contacts with all the parties concerned. The objective of these contacts would be to ascertain the position of the various parties with respect to the principles set out in this declaration and in the light of the results of this consultation process to determine the form which such an initiative on their part could take.

The two main points of the Declaration were Point 6: ". . . to exercise fully its right to self-determination," and Point 7: ". . . the PLO, which will have to be associated with the negotiations." One should point out that the Community steered away from mentioning a Palestinian state, an exclusive PLO role, or the need for a new UN resolution. However, the following day the *Daily Telegraph* asserted that: "The Nine have moved significantly towards the Palestinians and away from unfettered support for Israel."

Israel's reaction to the Declaration was harsh. At the 15 June regular cabinet meeting a communiqué, which Menahem Begin himself had drawn up, was approved:

The decision calls upon us and other nations to be involved in the peace process, to bring in the Arab SS—called the Palestinian Liberation Organisation.

The major component of this murderous organization decided in Damascus, on the eve of the Venice gathering, that its aim was to liberate Palestine completely, and to liquidate the Zionist entity, politically, economically, militarily, culturally and ideologically.

Since *Mein Kampf* was written no words were ever more explicit for all the world to hear, Europe included, on the striving to destroy the Jewish State and nation.

For the peace that would be achieved with the participation of that organisation of murderers, a number of European countries are prepared to give guarantees, even military ones.

Anyone with a memory must shudder, knowing the result of that guarantee given to Czechoslovakia in 1938 after the Sudetenland was stolen from it, also in the name of self-determination.

Israel asks for no security guarantees from any European people. Israel does know how to defend itself.

The initiators of the Venice document also sought to interfere with the status of Jerusalem our eternal and our right to settle and live in the land of Israel, a right that is an integral part of our national security in face of enemies and aggressors:

Any man of good will and every free person in Europe who studies the document will see in it a Munich surrender, the second in our generation, to totalitarian blackmail and an encouragement to all those elements which seek to undermine the Camp David agreements and bring about the failure of the peace process in the Middle East.[78]

The reference to Munich should be noted as it was made after the Israeli prime minister frequently inveighed against the attitude of the Europeans during the Second World War in the weeks that preceded the Venice meeting: Begin repeatedly accused the countries of Western Europe of having "collaborated with the Nazis during the war" and of having been "passive" while the Jews were being exterminated. Such accusations had been angrily rejected by the European governments but were certainly bound to please Israeli public opinion. Before the cabinet meeting, the prime minister had originally drawn up a statement specifically attacking France and Germany. He was finally persuaded by other ministers not to name these two countries, but he refused to moderate his communiqué. Sources close to Begin said that he would certainly oppose any EEC fact-finding mission operating on the basis of the Venice statement.[79] (In 1979, Israel had actually refused to admit a UN mission investigating Jewish settlements in the territories.)

The Israeli government's irritation stemmed mainly from the two following factors: (1) the countries "friendly" to Israel in the EEC (Holland, Denmark and to a lesser extent, Germany) had done nothing to prevent such a resolution from being passed; (2) the United States had reacted so "tamely" to the Venice statement. As soon as it was issued, Edmund Muskie said that "he could see nothing in the text which directly challenges the Camp David process." Muskie added: "We are not trying to keep the PLO out . . . the negotiating base must be broadened at the right time." But for the time being, Muskie ruled out "specific participation" by the PLO in peace talks, unless it disavowed its goal of destroying Israel and accepted UN Security Council resolutions.[80] It is true that the Venice statement constituted the most satisfying foreign policy "compromise" that the Americans had obtained from the Europeans in a long time. As one US National Security Council official put it: "The Venice outcome avoided a dangerous gap appearing between us and the Europeans, and it might even be helpful in US efforts to get a settlement."[81]

However, this "passivity" acutely angered the Israelis.[82] In many European press editorials, we find the contention that Venice showed that the EEC leaders definitely had stopped trusting Begin, and that from that point they placed all their hopes in a Labor victory in the next Knesset elections. But the Israeli Labor Party's reaction was no less virulent than that of the Likud. According to Shimon Peres, the Venice Declaration "damages Europe first of all and reduces European influence on Israel and Middle Eastern countries which truly seek peace."[83] On the other hand, Israeli public opinion—used to paying attention only to developments in the Middle East, and to Washington's policy— showed complete indifference (one could say disdain) towards the European initiative.

Interestingly the PLO leadership expressed great disappointment. Of course, the Palestinians had scored a point, but the practical implications of Venice were far from evident. On 15 June the PLO issued a scathing assessment of the Declaration and it said it was "the product of American blackmail," full of contradictions and ambiguities. The PLO asserted that it represented a European attempt to save the Washington-sponsored Camp David Accords, and that the EEC had ignored the basic prerequisites for a just and durable peace in the Middle East, as well as the crux of the Arab-Israeli conflict.[84] A few days later, Arafat repeated that the statement was "inadequate." A Bir-Zeit University Palestinian intellectual, close to the PLO, explained why "the Palestinians are against the Venice Statement"; according to him, "There is very little to say about the Great Initiative." He explained that the Palestinians were hoping for a call at the UN to modify Resolution 242, a clear-cut assertion that the Camp David framework was inadequate, and that the PLO would be recognized as the sole representative of the Palestinians. All this had not happened. The Europeans had therefore purely aligned themselves with the US positions.[85] At the end of July 1980, speaking at the extraordinary session of the UN General Assembly, PLO representative Kaddoumi presented a scarcely more optimistic evaluation of Venice: he declared that although he perceived a "glimmer of hope" in the statement it was insufficient and in effect the Europeans had yielded to US blackmail.[86]

In all, the reaction of the main parties concerned with the Declaration— Israel and the PLO—was very negative, and this was one of the main reasons for the EEC's failure to implement the document. The only "encouragement" came from the "moderate" Arab countries, Jordan and Saudi Arabia. On a visit to Paris at the end of July 1980, Jordan's King Hussein declared: "[N]o one can deny that there has been a positive and very important development on Europe's part, in the right direction."[87] At the end of August 1980 Prince Fahd warned: "The European initiative is the last chance for a settlement to the Arab-Israeli conflict before the Arab countries use all the means they have at their disposal."[88]

The reaction of Egypt, which was deeply involved in the Camp David process, was more ambiguous, because it wanted to "keep two irons in the fire." Sadat did *not* openly take a stand in favor of the statement but, in contrast to Israel and the PLO, neither did he formally refute it.[89] Minister Butros-Ghali called the Declaration "a contribution to the peace process," and Egypt adopted a wait-and-see stance. If discussions on Palestinian autonomy progressed Sadat would ignore the European intervention; however if, as it turned out, negotiations with Israel ended in an impasse, Egypt would give the Venice Declaration its full support. In fact Egypt increasingly gave its support to the European initiative. This development was to be reinforced after Sadat's death and his replacement by Hosni Mubarak.

European Voting at the UN (1980)—
Implementation of the Venice Declaration

At the 1980 General Assembly session the Nine clearly tried to implement their Venice principles by adopting a common stance towards the Palestinian-Israeli conflict.

For example, the Nine unanimously voted in favor of Resolution 35/ 169E, which condemned the "Jerusalem Law" and declared this document void of any legal content; also they approved Resolution 35/122 A,B,D,E,F which supported the actions of the Special Committee of Inquiry on Israeli practices "violating human rights" in the occupied territories. And they supported Resolution 35/13E, which asked Israel to recognize the right of all Palestinian refugees who had left their homes in 1967 to return.

Together, the Nine abstained on important resolutions such as 35/ 169C on the activities of the Special Group on the Rights of the Palestinians, 35/122 I which criticized Israel's violations of the Geneva Convention, 35/122 E on Israeli practices in the Golan Heights and 35/122 F on Israeli "atrocities" against students and pupils in the territories. Finally they opposed Resolution 35/206 H which condemned Israeli collaboration with South Africa.

A comparison of European voting in 1980 with that in previous General Assembly sessions clearly indicates a greater degree of unity. There were only a few instances of deviation from this standard. France abstained on Resolutions 35/169 A and B while the other eight voted against against these texts. The first of these two documents spoke of the right of the Palestinian people to independence and sovereignty in Palestine, of their right to statehood, and of the PLO as "the" representative of the Palestinians. Resolution 35/169 B condemned negotiations which did not take into account the rights of the Palestinians (i.e. Camp David) and separate peace agreements (the Israeli-Egyptian treaty). In both cases, the French representatives at the UN preferred to follow Giscard's line in his spring declaration at Abu-Dhabi, rather than go along with their eight partners. And in two other cases, the Nine were strongly divided: on the main UN resolution on the Middle

East, 35/207, which was very critical of Israeli policies in almost every field, France, Ireland and Italy abstained, while the six others voted negatively; and on 35/157 (Israeli nuclear power), only Holland and Denmark did not accept the exclusive criticism contained in the text, while the seven others abstained. In conclusion, the General Assembly of 1980 witnessed two phenomena: on the one hand, the Venice Declaration encouraged increased European unity but on the other hand, it did not deprive the most pro-Arab (France, Italy, Ireland) and the most pro-Israeli countries (Denmark, Netherlands) of their will to act separately.

The Thorn Mission and Its Results

One of the main points of the Venice statement was that the Europeans would contact all the parties concerned, to enable the EEC to determine the form of a European initiative. The EEC would, therefore, dispatch a mission to the Middle East, led by Gaston Thorn of Luxemburg, who was President of the Council of Ministers for the second half of 1980. Although Thorn was said to have good relations with all the parties, there were some problems. First, Luxemburg hardly had the logistic and diplomatic basis in the Middle East to handle a mission of such scope. In addition, having been nominated future president to the EEC Commission beginning in January 1981, Thorn would not have much time to devote to his mission.

The Nature of the Thorn Mission

The Europeans first had to solve three basic questions:[90] (1) Would the mission limit itself to gathering facts and information, or should it also (as the Arabs wished) propose concrete solutions? It was the first option that was carried out. (2) On what level should the Thorn mission establish its contacts—governmental, parliamentary, opposition? It was decided that Thorn should try to appeal to the highest level of decision-makers; if possible to the Heads of State and Government, or ministers for foreign affairs. (3) Lastly, who would be involved in the talks of the Thorn mission? The basic problem was, obviously, one of knowing whether Thorn would meet with only representatives of states (as Israel required) or with the representatives of the PLO as well. This latter solution was chosen, as a seemingly natural consequence of the Venice Declaration. There would, therefore, be a Thorn-Arafat meeting, despite the reservations of the Dutch and the Danes.

The Atmosphere in Which the Mission Took Place

A number of problems created a rather strained atmosphere around the Thorn Mission. First, the mission took place at a time when the Community had many other urgent questions to resolve: the negotiations with Spain and Portugal, commercial relations with the US and Japan, anti-crisis measures for the steel industry, and the proposed regulations to implement the agreement reducing the UK's budget contributions. Furthermore, while the US had adopted a passive attitude to the Venice statement, it hardened its position during the presidential election campaign. Thus, Henry Kissinger, who—it was then thought—was to be one of the "strongmen" of a Reagan administration sharply attacked the Community's efforts in the Middle East.[91]

One of the main parties involved, Israel, toughened its policy. On 23 July 1980 the "Jerusalem Law" was passed, an event which precipitated the departure of European and other embassies from this city.[92] The Begin government had strongly criticized the Nine for having abstained on the Arab resolution at the extraordinary session of the UN on Palestine.[93] Israel viewed the anti-semitic outbursts in Antwerp and later on rue Copernic in Paris as concrete evidence that the European positions encouraged terrorism.

Finally, the Thorn mission was to take place during a major controversy engulfing the US, European political circles and Israel: namely whether Arafat and his al-Fatah organization were in the process of "moderating" themselves and moving towards conciliatory positions with regard to the Jewish state.

In fact, at the beginning of August 1980, at a time when Gaston Thorn was starting his tour of Middle East capitals, Arafat granted the *Herald Tribune* an interview in which he declared: "Reports that al-Fatah had called for the complete liberation of Palestine, and the liquidation of the Zionist entity politically, economically, militarily, culturally and ideologically were incorrect." He alleged that the text was only a draft resolution submitted by a small group in the PLO and had never been adopted by the PLO congress proper. Arafat's attempt to pass as a "moderate" was particularly significant since it occurred just a few days before the meeting he was to have with Thorn.[94] The pro-Arab groups in Europe followed suit and portrayed the Palestinian leader as moderate and conciliatory. Some European politicians were only too happy to be able to accept these appraisals while all this merely served to inflame Israeli-European relations.

Thorn's Two Trips to the Middle East

Gaston Thorn's first stop in the Middle East was Jerusalem. The results of his meetings with Israeli leaders were rather negative. He repeated that he had come "to listen" but the Israelis did not leave him with any illusions. They told him once more that it was out of the question to have the PLO associated with the peace process, in any way whatsoever.[95]

Thorn's second important meeting was in Beirut with Yasser Arafat. For the first time since Venice the Palestinian leader adopted a relatively positive attitude towards the European initiative, and he called on Europe to go further than simply passing resolutions and making speeches. He stated that he expected from the Europeans three specific steps: (1) That they should have UN Resolution 242 changed; (2) That they should explicitly recognize the Palestinians' right *to a state*; (3) And that they should recognize the PLO as the *only* legitimate representative of the Palestinians.[96]

During his second trip, at the end of August and the beginning of September 1980, the Luxemburg minister consulted with the Egyptians, and Sadat reiterated his increasingly favorable attitude to Europe.[97] Thorn wanted to visit Israel again but the hostile attitude of that country's government intensified and the second visit to Israel was cancelled for obscure reasons.[98] It was finally held at the end of September in a very unpleasant atmosphere. The EEC Council president had in the meanwhile committed the error (from the Israeli point of view) of sending Arafat a letter in which he wrote that "he shared his concern about the concentration of Israeli troops on the Lebanese border."[99] The atmosphere in which Thorn's second visit to Israel took place could be described only as "total disagreement."[100] It was at that very moment that the Israelis developed an argument aimed at countering European efforts in the Middle East.

According to Jerusalem, the Europeans, by concentrating all their efforts on the Palestinian problem, were neglecting the other urgent problems of the Middle East, such as the war between Iran and Iraq. Israel's ambassador to Great Britain, Shlomo Argov, put it thus:

- Once again, the world is alarmed by the possible consequences of a Middle East war: yet for once this is not another Arab/Israeli war but rather a bitter struggle between two Islamic countries: Iran and Iraq. At the other end of the Middle East, where Egypt and Israel lie, there is peace;
- But for months now European political councils have argued that the most pressing and urgent need was to provide a swift solution to the Palestinian problem;
- It seems to have mattered little that a framework for a genuine effort to resolve this problem has been hammered out at Camp David. . . . And so for months all available European political resources have been deployed in devising a Middle East policy with

little relevance to the pressing problems of the Gulf area and equally little regard for its possible counter-productive consequences in the Arab/Israeli sphere.[101]

The Results of the Thorn Mission

The inability of the Nine to draw any "conclusion" from the Thorn mission was a clear indication that it had failed to achieve any concrete result. No "initiative" emerged from Thorn's fact-finding trips to the Middle East and the problems of the region were relegated to the background. For example, in September 1980 the EEC ministers discussed Zimbabwe's problems at greater length than the Israeli-Arab conflict,[102] and at Echternach (25–26 October 1980) they merely skimmed over the problems of the Middle East while waiting for the American presidential election.[103] Lastly, one had hoped for a new European action at the Luxemburg European Council of December, but we shall see that this did not occur.

The Thorn missions had simply proven what had already been known for a long time: the positions of the two main parties—Israel and the PLO—were totally antithetical and irreconcilable. If the Europeans had thought they might be able to find some common denominator, some basis for an agreement between the positions of the two enemies, they were mistaken. We might add that the failure was not unexpected since the European initiative did not really introduce any new ideas into the tragic equation.

Furthermore, the Europeans had chosen to wait for the results of the American elections. These brought to power a new president, whose Middle East options were unknown—except for the fact that he was considered as a "strong supporter" of Israel. Several European countries were inclined to give Reagan the chance to work out his own Middle East policy, before going further on the path of a European initiative. They wanted to see if Reagan could and would develop a stand different from that of his predecessor.

Thus Lord Carrington announced in an interview published on 14 November 1980 in the *Herald Tribune* that Great Britain wanted to wait and, for the time being, to restrain EEC's efforts in the Middle East.[104] According to the interviewer the attitude of the British minister reflected his eagerness to start off on a good footing with the new American administration. The remarks attributed to Lord Carrington provoked an official French reply: "It is impossible to see how one can be an advocate of increased political cooperation, and at the same time declare that Europe should not make any initiative, nor let its activity become dependent on U.S. political developments."[105] The British were to deny the French accusations, but Lord Carrington declared, all the same, that he "was not expecting any major decision to emerge from the European Council meeting on the 1st of December. . . ."[106]

Finally, the EEC members hesitated to formulate a new policy in their Middle East efforts because of the growing disunity in the Arab world. The war between Iran and Iraq raged on; the Jordanians supported Iraq, while the Syrians supported Iran. On 25 November 1980, what came to be known as the "Arab Summit of Discord" was held in Amman. Lebanon, Egypt, and the five countries of the Rejection Front (Syria, Lybia, Algeria, South Yemen and the PLO) were not there.[107] Such a situation could only induce the Europeans to be very cautious.

The European Council of Luxemburg (1–2 December 1980) and the Middle East

In a leading article published in the *Times* at the time the European Council was taking place, former British Prime Minister Heath analyzed the reasons for the failure of European efforts since Venice.[108] He asserted that the Venice Declaration failed to insist explicitly on the morally and politically essential pre-condition for the association of the PLO with negotiations for a settlement: namely that the PLO must recognize Israel's right to exist behind at least its 1967 borders. Heath contended that this was a pre-condition not only for including the PLO in an ultimate settlement but also for involving it in any formal negotiations with Israel itself. In addition, Heath pointed out that "the Venice Declaration also failed to provide Israel with any credible assurance about the transitional arrangements which would be needed to ensure its security in the implementation of a settlement." The ex-prime minister declared that Europe did have an important role to play, but that it lacked a plan to accomplish this. A series of vague declarations on ultimate objectives did not constitute a strategy; strategy would only emerge if the foreign ministers and the heads of government of the EEC addressed themselves to the central problems. Among these Heath enumerated: (1) the meaning of "secure borders for Israel"; (2) the minimum acceptable definition of "legitimate rights for the Palestinians"; (3) the best way in which the Palestinian people could be represented in the negotiations; (4) how the PLO could be given an incentive for moderation; (5) the requirements of the traditional phases through which the process of peacemaking must pass before proceeding to an ultimate settlement.

The European Council of Luxemburg was not in a position to solve these basic problems. It produced a very neutral statement on the Middle East.

The Luxemburg Statement[109]

The European Council reviewed the action taken by the Nine since the adoption of the Venice Declaration on the Middle East.

The Council heard the report of Mr. Thorn on the mission which he carried out on behalf of the Nine in accordance with paragraph 11 of the Venice Declaration. It noted that this mission had made clear the great interest aroused by the position taken up by Europe and that in this respect it had been a success.

The results of the mission confirm that the principles of the Venice Declaration incorporate the essential elements for a comprehensive, just and lasting settlement to be negotiated by the parties concerned. They reinforce the Nine's determination to contribute to the search for such a settlement.

In this spirit the European Council approved the decision of the Ministers of Foreign Affairs to undertake consideration of the matter with the aim of clarifying and giving substance to the Venice principles. This consideration has resulted in the drafting of a report on the principal problems relating to a comprehensive settlement under the following headings: withdrawal, self-determination, security in the Middle East, Jerusalem.

The report emphasizes that the measures envisaged under these four headings should form a coherent whole and should therefore be co-ordinated carefully.

The European Council was in agreement on this approach.

It noted that different formulas were possible to give substance to some of the Venice principles, in particular on the duration of the transitional period leading up to the electoral procedure for self-determination, the definition of the provisional authority for the vacated territories, the conditions and modalities for self-determination, the guarantees of security, and Jerusalem.

With a view to a more thorough exploration of these formulas and with the determination to encourage a climate more favourable to negotiations, the European Council considered it necessary that new contacts be established with the parties concerned side by side with continued discussions within the Community.

The European Council accordingly instructed the Presidency-in-Office to undertake these contacts in consultation with the Ministers for Foreign Affairs.

The Council also asked the Ministers to continue their discussions with due regard for developments in the situation and to report back to the Council.

The European Council laid down this action programme in order to provide a more consistent platform designed to bring the parties concerned closer together.

Thus the text reviewed what the Nine had done since Venice, insisted on the "results" of the Thorn Mission (called a "success") and announced the Community's determination to continue its peace efforts. The statement declared that the EEC would continue to initiate contacts with the parties concerned which would be based on a document prepared in November 1980 by the directors for political affairs of the foreign ministries.[110] This document, which was to be kept confidential until the consultations could be resumed, was partly published in *Le Soir* of 27 December 1980. It contained a *list of options*, dealing with four topics: (1) Israeli withdrawal from all the occupied territories; (2) self-determination for the Palestinians; (3) securities and guarantees for Israel; (4) the status of Jerusalem. The nine countries proposed various solutions concerning these areas, but some very clear preferences were apparent from the text and the spirit in which it was drawn up was certainly designed to please the Arab world.

The publication of this document did not make the EEC's efforts easier. The German and Italian governments denied that this was actually the text,[111] but it became clear later that *Le Soir*'s article was, in fact, based on the truth. This list of options was completely revealed in March 1981[112] and it drew a strong reaction from the Israeli government. Mr. Begin warned: "This is a plan of making it possible one day to wipe out Israel, to completely change our national situation and to bring the greatest danger to our country."[113]

The Van der Klaauw Mission and Its Results

Before discussing the Van der Klaauw mission during the first months of 1981, one should point out a very important event which took place on 1 January 1981: the official entry of Greece into the European Community.

This was a significant development given the particularly strong relations which existed between Greece and Arab countries, and the fact that Athens had never recognized Israel *de jure* and maintained diplomatic relations only at a non-ambassadorial level. After 1 January 1981, there was a sudden "warming" in Israel-Greek relations, as though membership in a community of states which maintained normal relations with Israel had affected Greece "by osmosis." Between January and March 1981 Greece came closer to formally recognizing Israel and establishing full diplomatic relations.

On 9 January 1981, the director-general of the Israel Foreign Ministry, David Kimche, met in Athens with Foreign Minister Mitsotakis. The two discussed "bilateral issues," but concentrated on the problem of *de jure* recognition. Kimche described his conversations as "long, profound and fruitful."[114] He predicted that there would be more "openness" in future relations and that Greece would give greater weight to Israeli views, even if it did not agree with them. In May 1981 Greek Minister of Agriculture Kanellopoulos came on an official visit to Israel and the warm remarks which he made in Jerusalem pleased the surprised Israelis. At the same time, Mitsotakis accorded an interview to *Le Monde* in which he stated: "We do not have regular diplomatic relations with Israel, nor ambassadors. We plan to normalize this situation as soon as the opportunity arises. Our entry into the community might have provided such an occasion, but circumstances were not favorable. . . . Let us hope for a change after the Israeli elections."

Arab states reacted sharply to what appeared to be an Israeli-Greek rapprochement. The ambassadors of five Arab countries—Saudi Arabia, Syria, Libya, Lebanon and Kuwait—demanded a meeting with Mitsotakis "to express their anxiety over a possible change in Greek policy." The ambassadors clearly stated that the Arabs, who supplied 80% of Greece's oil, were ready to use all the means at their disposal—especially the oil weapon—to prevent Greek recognition of Israel. Mitsotakis had to assure the ambassadors that the rumors were false, that Greece would not recognize Israel. The "honeymoon" between Greece and Israel had come to an end.

During the first six months of 1981, during which the Netherlands held the presidency of the EEC, a number of elements and circumstances prevented any new European initiative from taking off the ground.

In the first place, despite the fact that the presidency was held by Holland—the country with the greatest reservations towards including the PLO in the peace process, and still Israel's best friend in the EEC—there was little progress. Van der Klaauw repeatedly declared that he did *not* intend "spectacular new steps." In fact, the Dutch wanted to keep as low a profile as possible. The Arabs hoped that there would be a change in the second part of the year, when the presidency would be passed to Great Britain. But, in the interim, other events were to occur.

In the second place, the new American administration took a long time to define its Middle East policy. And, as long as it had not been defined, the Americans continued to insist that their European allies, and especially the Thatcher government, not take any initiative in the Middle East.

This hostility toward any independent European effort was voiced in January 1981 by Henry Kissinger (even if he spoke only as a private citizen). In Jerusalem Kissinger stated: "Europe must play a more active part, but I think that its efforts must be connected with those of the United States. There could be two different and correct approaches, but Europe must not hinder American attempts. It is unthinkable that the US and Europe should have a common defense policy and different foreign policies."[115] On his return from the United States in February

1981, the Italian Minister Colombo confirmed to his European colleagues that he had the distinct impression that the Americans (especially the Congress) were reticent about any new initiative by the Europeans.[116] In fact, the Reagan administration was to become increasingly hostile to any intimation of an independent European initiative. In response, on 27 February, while visiting Washington, Prime Minister Thatcher reassured that "the European initiative was *not* intended to compete with the negotiations being carried out under the auspices of the US."[117]

A third reason for the failure of European efforts was linked to the two important elections which were held in 1981: the first in one of the main countries of the EEC, France, and the second in the country most concerned by the initiative, Israel.

Giscard d'Estaing had been the foremost supporter of an independent European intervention in Middle East affairs, and had expressed strong reservations about Camp David. By contrast, Mitterand was considered a staunch friend of Israel, and had been one of the foremost European supporters of Camp David.[118] During the French presidential campaign Mitterand stressed his image as a pro-Israeli statesman in order to win the "Jewish vote" and Giscard d'Estaing put aside his pro-Arab sympathies and stopped attacking the Camp David process.

The political situation in France was therefore not conducive to the development of the European initiative in the shape it had thus far assumed. And when Mitterand was elected, many people thought that the initiative had come to an end and that France would oppose any continuation of European efforts based on the Venice Declaration.

In the same way, the Israeli elections held on 30 June 1981 had been an obstacle to a continued initiative for at least for three reasons: First, because it was expected that the Labor Party could win, the Europeans wanted to avoid doing anything which could be interpreted as hostile, and which might turn the Israeli public away from "moderation." Knowing how unpopular their efforts were in Israel, the Europeans agreed to "tone down" their initiative. In addition, Menahem Begin, playing on his voters' admiration of his "strongman" image, of a man who knows "how to answer back to foreign governments," and recognizing that most Israelis were disdainful of Europe, increased his attacks against Europe and the EEC during the campaign. These attacks culminated in his sharp criticism of Giscard d'Estaing and Schmidt's "greediness." Finally, the Labor party itself reiterated its public attacks against the European plans. In January 1981 Shimon Peres undertook a tour of European capitals to tell the Europeans "how totally his party was opposed to Venice and the initiative."[119] In March 1981 Abba Eban—then thought to be the next foreign minister—described the European initiative as "the principal obstacle to peace moves in the region." He said that: "The idea that European armed forces would go and fight Arabs—even in the event of flagrant violations of the Israeli borders— is too ludicrous to even consider."[120] Nevertheless, EEC governments hoped for a little more "flexibility" when the Labor party would assume office. They were certainly disappointed when the Israeli electorate brought Mr. Begin back to power.

Finally, the Arabs who had everything to gain from a European initiative, did nothing to help it get off the ground. The disunity shown at the Amman Summit continued and even increased. Every camp wanted to be perceived as "tougher" than the others.

Thus, while the preparations of the Euro-Arab dialogue were resumed in November 1980—the Europeans had even agreed to sit at the same table with the PLO president of the Arab delegation[121]—the ministerial meeting planned for mid-1981 was continually delayed. The Arabs wanted the Community to recognize the PLO as the sole representative of the Palestinians before the ministerial meeting. But it was too much to ask, at this stage, and the ministerial meeting did not take place.

Moreover, the PLO and the Arab states of the Rejection Front were furious at the signs of support shown to Egypt, such as the warm welcome given to President Sadat at the European Parliament,[122] the passage of a resolution sympathetic to Egypt, and the Parliament's request that Egypt be associated with the Euro-Arab dialogue.[123]

The PLO expressed increasingly negative feelings towards the European initiative. In January 1981 Arafat declared: "Who said there had been a European initiative? Nobody talked about it. What there was was a political statement, at the time of the Venice Summit. But above all what there was was a statement made by Secretary of State Muskie affirming that the US would never authorize a European initiative. . . ."[124] Then, on the eve of the Van der Klaauw mission Arafat proclaimed: "Europe must make it quite clear that it will not give in to American pressure. We need a tangible decision."[125] When the European Parliament asked Egypt to become associated with the dialogue, the PLO declared: "It is an unacceptable interference in the internal affairs of the Arab world."[126]

At the very moment when Van der Klaauw met with Yasser Arafat on 20 April, the PLO adopted a "hard" line: the Palestinian leader told the Dutch minister that the PLO had already made too many concessions, and at the same time he arranged for the National Palestinian Council, which was meeting concurrently, to issue a call "to rally all the Arab fronts for operations against Israel." The National Palestinian Council gave also a warm welcome to Brezhnev's proposals on the Middle East.[127] The EEC was encouraged only by Egypt's increasingly positive attitude towards its efforts, an attitude which was noted by Lord Carrington during his Cairo visit in January 1981,[128] and which was also displayed by Sadat in his address to the European Parliament.

The Kris Van der Klaauw mission to the Middle East which began in Damascus on 22 February 1981 therefore took place under unfavorable conditions. Despite his deep desire to be constructive and achieve something new, the Dutch minister was only able to repeat what his predecessors had done. Already in March 1981, *Europe* could observe that: "Van der Klaauw's trip to the Middle East does not seem to have come in with anything new to add to the European initiative. The response was evasive and full of scepticism."[129] The minister's visit to Israel was just as unfruitful. Israeli radio said that "the talks were very tough,"[130] and Begin accused Europe—once more—of "claiming to know what was good for Israel's security, while overlooking the massacring of Christians in Lebanon." On leaving Israel, the minister could only say: "There is still no prospect of a European initiative . . ."[131]

The European Council, held on 20–30 June 1981 in Luxemburg, analyzed the results of the Van der Klaauw mission but could only observe the impracticability of a concrete European action on the Palestinian question. The Luxemburg statement on the Middle East added nothing new to the Venice Declaration and the Council confined itself to asking the foreign ministers to study the various options and possibilities. In addition, it recalled the Community's support for the Security Council Resolution condemning the Israeli raid in Iraq.[132] As an editorial pointed out: "the initiative, already a sickly creature before the Summit emerged from that meeting with few signs of life."[133]

The 30 June 1981 Statement on the Middle East

The European Council noted the report of the Presidency as well as Mr. Van der Klaauw's oral comments on his contacts with the parties concerned with the Middle East conflict.

It concluded that the efforts undertaken by the Ten to promote the conclusion of a peaceful settlement would be continued energetically and without respite, taking account of the results of the missions decided upon in Venice.

Accordingly, the European Council decided, on the basis of the results of the mission just completed by the President-in-Office, to instruct Ministers to elaborate further the practical possibilities available to Europe to make an effective contribution towards a comprehensive peace settlement in the Middle East, through internal reflection, appropriate contacts being maintained with all parties concerned, including the United States.

As regards the attack by the Israeli air force on the Iraqi nuclear plant on 7 June 1981 the European Council can only endorse the Resolution adopted unanimously by the UN Security Council.

The Absence of Any Further Initiative, from the End of the Van der Klaauw Mission (July 1981) to the War in Lebanon (June 1982)

From the time Lord Carrington took over the presidency of the EC, new circumstances prevented any significant European action in the Israeli-Arab conflict. For example, Menachem Begin put together a cabinet which had a stronger nationalistic character than the previous one (the moderate component of the previous coalition, Yigal Yadin's Movement for Democratic Change, no longer existed); the PLO continued to be intransigent, after the hard-line decisions made at the Palestinian National Council; tensions were being exacerbated, in particular in Lebanon, where the Syrians were stationing missiles, and where the Israelis were bombing; there was an international oil glut which minimized the risk of pressure by the Arab oil states on the Europeans.

Beyond these circumstances, five other elements enable us to understand the absence of any European initiative in the year which preceded the war in Lebanon.

1. The occurrence of three landmark events: Sadat's assassination; Israel's complete withdrawal from Sinai; and the Falklands crisis.

Just as Lord Carrington (who had played a major role in generating the initiative) was preparing to renew his diplomatic efforts, Egypt's president was assassinated. It was necessary to wait, at least several weeks, until his successor defined his own attitudes toward the American and European approaches.

Since the beginning of 1982, everyone was waiting for Israel's withdrawal from Sinai. Many Europeans thought, as they had before the 1981 Knesset elections, that if external powers such as the EEC were too "radical" or "aggressive" towards Israel, they could contribute to a negative decision by the Israeli government. Fearing that the Israelis would finally decide *not* to withdraw, the Europeans did nothing.

Just before Israel's withdrawal in April 1982 the Falklands crisis, which involved one of the major European powers, diverted the EC's attention from Middle East affairs.

Two months later, the war in Lebanon began. Between these events, the European Community was obliged to take a wait-and-see attitude, for these were *not* propitious circumstances for furthering the initiative formulated at Venice.

2. While Giscard d'Estaing's France had been the driving force behind European efforts in the Middle East and had directed the EEC towards an increasing support for the Palestinians, Mitterand's France seemed much more uncertain and irresolute regarding the Israeli-Arab conflict.

The new French government's first year was characterized by a series of zig-zags and about faces on Middle East matters. For example, speaking to the PLO's Faruk Kaddoumi in July 1981, the new foreign minister, Claude Cheysson, said that France would never condemn Camp David and would certainly refuse to consider the PLO as the sole representative of the Palestinians.[134] But in August 1981, Cheysson met Yasser Arafat in Beirut. At the end of their discussions, the content of which were kept secret, Yasser Arafat expressed his satisfaction and described the talks as "very constructive."[135] Then on his official visit to Israel in December, Cheysson declared: "There is no French plan [on the Middle East] and, as long as we are in government, there will be no European plan or European initiative." Cheysson declared in a radio interview that the adoption of a position against Camp David in the Venice Declaration "had been a mistake." (He was even said to have added that this declaration was an "absurdity.")[136] Cheysson's remarks delighted his Israeli hosts, startled European diplomats, and provoked harsh reactions in the Arab countries.[137] Afterwards, the minister said that "he regretted the interpretation made of certain of his remarks, as well as the way they were distorted: I never called the Venice Declaration mistaken or absurd."[138] He even added that the Venice Declaration "suits France's interests perfectly," but he made a distinction between this declaration and a mere initiative "from which there was nothing to expect."[139]

Then on a visit to Cairo in January 1982 Cheysson said that the Venice statement belonged to the past, because "from now on we are talking of a Palestinian State,"[140] and in Abu-Dhabi he said that "France does not know of any Palestinians other than the PLO, who would be ready to take part in peace negotiations."[141]

Soon after came a new "pro-Israeli" swing, with the visit of Francois Mitterand to Israel in March 1982. In his address to the Knesset, he adopted a much more moderate position than had Cheysson, and did not bring up at all the question of the PLO. He truly seemed to have abandoned any idea of a "mediation" by France and by Europe.

We shall see that a firm French policy was formulated only during the war in Lebanon. Until then the uncertainty regarding French policy led France's partners to the logical conclusion that no joint initiative could be renewed at the moment.

3. A completely new element was introduced with the publication of the Fahd plan in August 1981. For the first time (except for Sadat's initiative) an Arab country proposed a plan which, despite its ambiguity, seemed to contain an implicit or potential recognition of Israel.

The Europeans were very hesitant regarding what attitude to adopt: how could they reconcile the Fahd and the Venice plans? At their political

cooperation meeting of 13 October 1981 the foreign ministers decided
to pay special attention to the Saudi Arabian plan,[142] and their support
for it increased as time went on. Lord Carrington welcomed Fahd's
step as "extremely positive." The British minister went to Ryiad in
November 1981, hoping that "the Saudis would spell out more specifically
their willingness to give some recognition to Israel,"[143] but he was
disappointed. Carrington's enthusiasm for the plan reinforced Israel's
hostility to the European efforts, and even the American government
felt that Lord Carrington had gone too far.[144] The ten Europeans, who
had openly given their support to Fahd's plan, were very embarrassed
when the Arab Summit at Fez squarely rejected it, at the instigation of
the Syrians and the PLO.[145]

4. Among the reasons for the absence of joint European efforts, one
should mention pressures exerted by the Reagan administration, which
attempted to bring the EEC into the Israeli-Egyptian peace process. In
October 1981 the US proposed that the Europeans join the Multinational
Force and Observers (MFO) in the Sinai. The MFO was a direct result
of the Egyptian-Israeli Peace Treaty: on 18 May 1981 Egypt and Israel
had concluded a draft agreement on the MFO, which resulted on 3
August 1981 in an Egyptian-Israeli protocol witnessed by the US. The
US committed itself to supplying a considerable part of the required
troops and finances, to finding replacements for contingents that withdrew,
and to assuming the primary responsibility for approaching potential
contributors.

Only four EEC member states finally agreed to participate in the
MFO—France, Britain, Italy and Holland[146]—which, in itself, constituted a sign of division within the Community (one of the members,
Greece, did everything it could to thwart this European participation).
There were very strong reactions from the PLO and the Arab world:
participation in the MFO seemed to be a "surrender" to the Camp
David process.[147] The four European countries sought to justify their
participation in the MFO on the basis of their Venice Declaration,[148]
but Israel energetically rejected such an "interpretation" of the MFO;
from Israel's point of view, it could only be based on Camp David.[149]
Finally, the Europeans were obliged to yield and, after a two-month
controversy, they admitted that their participation would be founded
"on the various agreements between Egypt and Israel."[150] Division within
the Community, tension with the Arab world, and recognition of the
Camp David basis of their participation in the MFO, impeded European
efforts to further an independent initiative.

5. In the elections of 19 October 1981, Papandreou's party (the
PASOK) won 40% of the vote and 172 seats in the parliament, and
Papandreou formed a government based solely upon his party.[151] It is

true that the former party in power, the New Democracy of Caramanlis and Rallis, had not been very supportive of Israel. But as soon as he took power, Papandreou showed his deep hostility towards the Jewish state and tried to use the Community as a tool for his pro-Palestinian policy. In his first foreign policy address before the new Greek parliament in November 1981, Papandreou reaffirmed his government's "determination to broaden traditional relations with the Arab nation and support for the Palestinian struggle for self-determination."[152] Some days after the election the Greek prime minister invited Yasser Arafat to come to Athens on an official visit, announcing that on this occasion the PLO's information bureau would be elevated to the level of a "diplomatic representation."[153] This invitation was not preceded by any consultation with Greece's partners in the Community. Subsequently, one of the first steps taken by Papandreou in the sphere of foreign policy was to try to prevent the other members of the EEC from sending forces to the MFO.[154] When the European participation was discussed by the Community's Council of Ministers in late 1981, Foreign Minister Haralambopoulos opposed it because, according to him, Greece did not wish to be associated in any way whatsoever with the Camp David process. Thus, for the first time since the beginning of European political cooperation, a "joint foreign policy statement" was signed by only part of the member states (nine). Greece ultimately agreed to the issuing of two declarations, one by the four countries participating in the MFO and the second by the Ten, the latter making no mention of Camp David. Papandreou said that he would never approve any declaration which appeared to imply even indirect acceptance of Camp David.

The extremist policy of the new Greek government, its defiance towards the EEC, its harsh opposition to Camp David and its refusal to upgrade diplomatic relations with Israel, made it very difficult for the Community to undertake any mediation in the Middle East.

The attitude of the new Greek government and its refusal to make any compromises with other EEC member states was well reflected in the European voting pattern at the 1981 General Assembly. This session was marked by two opposite phenomena within the European camp. On the one hand, Greece's voting at the UN reflected her pro-Arab hard line. But on the other hand, Mitterand's victory in France softened Paris' positions on the Middle East and created a stronger will than before to coordinate French voting at the UN with the other EEC countries.

At the 1981 General Assembly session the Nine generally voted together, while Greece voted differently. Two important resolutions were 36/120F (condemnation of separate peace agreements) and 36/226A (strong and total condemnation of Israel). In both cases Greece voted in favor of the texts, the Nine against. In other instances Greece voted in favor of resolutions on which the Nine abstained. The latter was the most regular voting pattern and was exhibited, for example, on 36/27 (condemning Israel for the bombing of "Tamuz" nuclear plant), 36/120A,B,C (supporting the Committee on the Rights of the Palestinians), 36/226B (condemning the "Golan Law"), 36/87B and 36/98 (on Israeli nuclear power), 36/146B,C,G, 36/147C,F, 36/73, etc. Nevertheless, we even find cases when all ten European countries voted in the same manner: they voted in favor of R. 36/120E (condemning the "Jerusalem Law"); R. 36/146A (on the Gaza Strip refugees), F and H; and in particular they supported R. 36/147 A,B,C,D,E,G (affirming the report of the UN Special Committee of Inquiry on Israeli practices affecting human rights in the occupied territories). They also unanimously condemned Israel for its Med-Dead Sea project, which would partially cross the territories (R. 36/150). In some cases the Ten abstained (which reflected some kind of "moderation" by Greece), for example, on the condemnation of Israeli archeological excavations (36/15) and on the condemnation of Israeli exploitation of natural resources in the territories (36/173). The only resolution on which the Ten split into three groups was 36/120D, a text which proclaimed the right of the Palestinian people not only to self-determination but also to statehood. In that case Belgium, Denmark, Italy, Luxemburg, Holland, Germany and Britain voted against, France and Ireland abstained, and Greece supported the text.

Thus Sadat's assassination, the wait for the Israeli withdrawal from Sinai, the Falklands crisis, the uncertainty of France's Middle East policy, the issuing of the Fahd plan, the participation of four European states in the MFO, and PASOK's victory in Greece had a cumulative effect and blocked any independent initiative of the EEC in the Middle East. Lord Carrington's term as president of the Council of Ministers of the EC (July–December 1981) was particularly disappointing. He failed in his efforts to inaugurate a new initiative, and his enthusiastic support for the Fahd plan led nowhere.

Leo Tindemans' term (January–June 1982) hardly produced better results. No new important declaration on the Middle East was adopted by the Ten. The Europeans limited themselves to condemning the Israeli government's policy on several occasions: they condemned Israeli raids, the annexation of the Golan Heights, the new settlements, the Israeli policy in the West Bank, etc. But these were only a series of reactions to specific events, not a cohesive policy.

On the eve of the war in Lebanon the possibility of renewing the European initiative was once more discussed. Douglas Hurd, the British minister of state at the Foreign Office told the Council of Europe's

Assembly that the EEC was on the verge of a new Middle East initiative. At the end of April and beginning of May, Leo Tindemans visited Kuwait, Saudi Arabia and Egypt. In each of these countries he found "great expectations" of a European initiative. At the end of May the Belgian foreign minister went to Israel.

The result of these last contacts before the Lebanon war was a thirty-five page document, which attempted to find a new way to implement the Venice Declaration, making it more acceptable perhaps to the Israeli government. The document was supposed to be submitted to the European Council in Brussels, but in the interim the war in Lebanon broke out.

THREE

The European Community and the War in Lebanon (June 1982–June 1983)

From the Start of Israeli Offensive to the Evacuation of Beirut by the PLO

The First Shock

The Lebanese war broke out while the leaders of the seven richest countries in the West were holding a summit conference at Versailles, including the heads of four member states of the EEC: France, Great Britain, Germany and Italy. The entry of Israeli forces into Lebanon came barely hours after the Security Council called for "the cessation of all military activity" and just before Philip Habib's arrival in the Middle East.

All the participants in the Versailles summit, preoccupied by the Falklands crisis and the Iran-Iraq conflict, were surprised by the scope of the new operation, and the declaration which they issued was not fully coherent:

> We are overcome by the news which has reached us from Lebanon. We are deeply moved by the loss of human life and by the suffering and destruction. We think that this new cycle of violence could have, if it continues, disastrous consequences for the entire region.
>
> The Seven firmly support the appeals of the Security Council for an immediate and simultaneous cessation of violence. Each of our governments will use all the means at its disposal to achieve that goal.[155]

From the European point of view, the first two weeks of the war were characterized by confusion and indecision. Of course the "invasion"

71

was condemned, and the members of the EEC who sat on the Security Council voted for the resolutions of 7 June (one proposed by Japan, the other by Ireland) calling for a cease-fire. But they did not go much further. The fact that Israel should have a certain "security zone" free of terrorists on its northern border—the famous "40–45 kilometers" proclaimed by the Israeli Prime Minister—was, if not explicitly acknowledged, at least understood by the Europeans (who, furthermore, were shocked by the assassination attempt against Ambassador Argov). On the other hand, after a while the Ten began taking notably divergent attitudes.

Some countries strongly opposed Israel's actions. Britain adopted a "hard" position. Pointing out that the blacklist found on one of the London terrorists also included the name of Nabil Ramlawy, chief of the PLO delegation, the Thatcher government lent credence to the idea that the PLO had *not* been responsible for the assassination attempt (and that therefore the intervention in Lebanon was unjustified).[156] Ireland actively participated in the drive in the Security Council to condemn Israel. In no European country did the war give rise to such a collective anti-Israel hysteria as in Greece, both on the governmental level and that of the political parties, the media and the public. Greece launched a powerful campaign against Israel, completely aligning itself with the PLO. Having expressed its "shock and dismay," the Greek government demanded an immediate meeting of the EEC Council of Ministers to determine the sanction to be taken against the "aggressor."[157] Papandreou described the Israeli action as a "crime against humanity" declaring: "We live in a terrifying era. We have seen what Nazism did to Jews and now Jews are doing the same to Palestinians. Israel will have to respond and is responsible to history and to humanity; one day she will have to answer for these crimes."[158] In contrast, Germany, Holland, Luxemburg, Denmark, and Italy kept a low profile. France, which generally took the leading role in European initiatives and which at the time, held the presidency of the Security Council, seemed rather confused.[159] Despite obvious disenchantment with Israel, Francois Mitterand had sought to reestablish polite, even cordial, relations with that country and had visited Jerusalem in March. In Versailles Mitterand therefore condemned Israel in vague terms and expressed his "deep reprobation," but he was hesitant to go beyond that and run the risk of being rejected by Israel as a valid interlocutor and mediator as had been his predecessor, Giscard d'Estaing. Therefore Mitterand, while condemning Israel, was careful to emphasize that he "had not hesitated to condemn the other military interventions on Lebanese soil [as well], whenever they were made against the will of the Lebanese government."

Mitterand's indecisiveness was immediately noted by *Le Monde* which, in an editorial dated 9 June entitled "France on the Spot," suggested that the president's condemnation of Israel "had not come to his lips spontaneously," and observed an "absence of clarity" in his remarks. Similarly, a representative of the Arab League, Mohammed Yazid, stated that he was "disappointed by France's attitude" and linked that "vagueness" to Mitterand's spring trip to Israel.[160] The Arab leaders seemed shocked by Mitterand's remark that Lebanon, occupied by the Israelis, "was already occupied by two other armies, that of the Syrians and that of the Palestinians." That expression seemed to indicate a parallel between those "occupations," whereas Syria was in Lebanon as part of the peace-keeping force of the Arab League, and the presence of the PLO was accepted by the Lebanese agreements of 1969 (even if they were frequently violated).

In that climate of confusion and indecision the foreign ministers of the Ten met in Bonn on 9 June to formulate a joint declaration. The day before, the heads of the Arab diplomatic missions in Brussels had appealed to the Community to take effective measures:

"The moral force" represented by the position of Western Europe as expressed in the Venice Declaration has faded. . . . It was neither logical nor moral for Europe to be satisfied with merely following events from a distance. Ethics as well as its interests demanded of Europe that it intervene directly and take coercive measures to force the immediate evacuation of Israeli forces from Lebanon, and to make possible the beginning of a real, global peace process involving all the concerned parties, including the PLO, and regarding the rights of the Palestinian people to an independent and sovereign state on Palestinian soil.[161]

The differences among the European countries became evident during that meeting. After two hours of discussions they condemned the invasion of Lebanon "which is a flagrant violation of international law and which can only make the search for a solution to the conflict in the Middle East more difficult."[162] But when the Greeks demanded sanctions against Israel the other members refused, some saying that one must also condemn "every act of violence which makes a solution difficult." Apart from the condemnation in principle, there was no agreement except to offer humanitarian assistance to the victims and to continue working for "a just and durable solution to the conflict."[163] Ten days later in Luxemburg the representatives of the Ten demanded the following assurances from the Israeli government:

1. That it will admit international relief organizations to the territory occupied by its forces and facilitate their work.

2. Similarly that it will admit representatives of the press and allow them normal facilities.
3. That it will apply the Geneva conventions, particularly with regard to prisoners.
4. That it recognizes the sovereignty of the State of Lebanon and the international border between Lebanon and Israel.
5. That it desires neither to annex nor to occupy any part of Lebanese territory.
6. That it will not intervene in the internal affairs of Lebanon.
7. That it will cooperate fully with the Secretary General of the United Nations in every area of his responsibility.
8. That it has no hostile intention towards the Palestinian people.
9. That it has no offensive intentions against the neighboring countries, including Syria.
10. That it intends to observe the cease-fire which was instituted, if all the other combatants in the region do the same.

For its part, the European Parliament adopted a very moderate "emergency resolution," condemning equally the Israeli operation and all the terrorist acts previously launched against Israel. In that resolution, the result of a compromise among the center and center-right parties of the Parliament (Christian Democrats, Gaullists, Liberals, and Conservatives), the Assembly called for the retreat of all non-Lebanese armed forces from Lebanon and for negotiations among the concerned parties.

The Radicalization of the French Position and Its Influence on the Position of the EEC.

The change in the attitude of President Mitterand and his closest advisors—most prominently the minister of foreign affairs, Claude Cheysson, ocurred during the second week and became stronger during the third week of the conflict and was directly linked to Israel exceeding its first declared objectives and the blockade of Beirut. That change must be viewed in the context of French attitudes towards the United States and the PLO.

It is no exaggeration to say that Mitterand and his government had never placed a great deal of confidence in the Reagan administration. This mistrust, manifest from the time Mitterand assumed office, covered widely diverse strategic and economic areas. In the case of the Middle East, the French became convinced that Washington had—tacitly—given Begin the green light to launch his offensive in Lebanon, and especially that General Haig had agreed in advance to exceeding the 45 kilometer limit. The Americans' extremely moderate attitude towards Israel, their refusal to condemn forcibly the bombardment and the blockade, as well as their veto of the Security Council resolutions, gave final reinforcement to the French analysis. The United States also seemed to have "accepted" the Israeli occupation of Lebanon quite quickly and stopped demanding "unconditional" Israeli retreat. They appeared to agree with Begin that Israel should withdraw only when the Syrians and Palestinians had left. At that point Mitterand wished to "denounce" that American-Israeli "conspiracy," formed without consulting the Europeans.

In addition, there was Mitterand's personal analysis of the Palestinian problem and the role of the PLO. In 1981 the French president had rejected the Venice conference and the European initiative because the latter was "unbalanced" and he felt that a climate of confidence had to be reestablished with Israel before Europe could play any role in the Middle East. Therefore he undertook his voyage of "reconciliation" to Israel. But his wish to renew ties with Israel was associated with the belief that the Palestinian problem was in fact the center of the conflict, and that the "moderate leadership of the PLO" around Yasser Arafat definitely had a role to play in peace negotiations. The Mitterand team had always insisted on what it considered to be the fundamental division between "extremists" and "moderates" within the PLO: whereas nothing was possible with the "extremists" (Habbash, Hawatmeh, Jibrill, etc.), high hopes could be held for the "moderates" grouped around Arafat. (One should note here that in France it was largely Dr. Issam Sartawi who created the image of a moderate group within the PLO leadership. His meetings in Paris with members of the Israeli left, such as Arieh Eliav, evoked very positive responses in France, especially among the Socialists.) In any case, since the French Socialist government considered mutual recognition by the PLO and Israel to be a basic policy objective, the "moderates" in the PLO were of primary importance in the Socialist party strategy.

During the intensive bombardment of western Beirut and the blockade, with the steady advance of Israeli troops, it appeared that the entire PLO, including its "moderates," was in danger of being crushed and annihilated. In Paris the prospect of a massive attack on western Beirut and the liquidation of the PLO leadership was not considered inconceivable. At that point it appeared that the "moderate" leadership of the PLO which was trapped in Beirut had to be "rescued" at any price, and that in a more general sense the complete destruction of the PLO had to be prevented. In the view of the French leadership, the destruction of the PLO could only lead to the subsequent rebirth of another Palestinian organization, even more extremist and entirely devoted to terrorism.

One must also add that while that analysis had already been elaborated among the President's team of advisors *before* the Israeli offensive, it was reinforced by the propitious climate created in France by that war. The media covered the "horrors" of Beirut incessantly, comparing West

Beirut to the Warsaw Ghetto, and an overtly pro-Palestinian attitude was assumed by the circles and groups which were traditionally linked with the French Socialist government. Mitterand found himself under intense pressure from Socialist party militants and certain ministers (Chevenement, Jobert, Rocard) who wanted him to quickly adopt a "hard" position against Israel. The division between pro-Israeli and pro-Arab factions within the leadership of the Socialist party was more and more pronounced and this time the pro-Arab group won. The French Communist party, with its four ministers, was entirely devoted to the cause of the PLO as well and placed pressure on Mitterand from the very start, in part through the Confederation Generale du Travail.

Thus a paradox soon developed: whereas Great Britain, which had sponsored the European initiative in 1980, fell silent and became passive, Mitterand, who had denounced the Venice initiative after his election, became the advocate of actual European intervention in Middle Eastern affairs. The change in tone became palpable with Foreign Minister Shamir's trip to Paris on 15 June (although the fact that the minister had been received by Mitterand was presented as a "success" in Israel at the time).[164] The French president was quite severe: he reaffirmed to Shamir "the solemn appeal launched by France that an end be put without delay to the bombardments, to the combat, and to the suffering of the Lebanese and Palestinian populations," and he recalled "the demand for the immediate withdrawal of Israeli armed forces from Lebanon, a demand already made by the Security Council and by the Ten." For his part Foreign Minister Cheysson emphasized to Shamir that France considered the invasion as a "violation of international law," and that it was clear that "without a normal future for the Palestinian people, a durable peace would not be possible in the Middle East." In Vienna the following day Mitterand declared, "International law is determined by the common accord of nations. No matter what objection one may make to that law, no one should substitute his sole decision and actions for the principles that govern the equilibrium of the world."[165]

Contacts between France and the PLO suddenly became more intense: first the Secretary of the Quai d'Orsay travelled to Beirut, then Farouk Kaddumi arrived in Paris and held discussions with the major French ministers. From that point all the foreign representatives of the PLO changed their approach and became very cordial towards France: "The French attitude is very positive," "There is a qualitative evolution in the relations between the PLO and the Socialist Party," they declared.[166]

Paris' intervention in the conflict in order to "salvage the PLO" became quite concrete in the statement published by Mitterand on 24 June, during the siege of Beirut:

Everything leads us to fear that, during the coming hours, tragic combats in Beirut itself will be added to the suffering already endured by the peoples of Lebanon.

The assault and destruction of the capital of Lebanon would compromise, painfully and in a permanent manner, the future of the entire country and of peace throughout the region.

France solemnly requests of Israel to respect the conditions of the cease-fire.

It is indispensable and urgent that disengagement be effectuated between all the forces presently in combat in West Beirut and its periphery, and that the Lebanese army be permitted to place itself between them, supported, if the legitimate government so desires, by a force constituted under the aegis of the Security Council.

Thus the neutralization of West Beirut could be obtained under the supervision of United Nations observers.

That would be the first step in the restoration of the authority of the Lebanese state in its territory. France is prepared, within the framework of the Security Council . . . to offer its cooperation in any efforts which the Lebanese government may decide.[167]

The five essential points of that text are: (1) fear that Israel would attack West Beirut; (2) specific condemnation of Israel for not respecting the cease-fire; (3) the demand for disengagement; (4) the demand for neutralization; (5) and the appeal to the Security Council. This statement was of course denounced by Israel with the same forcefulness with which it was immediately approved by the PLO leadership.

It is important to note that this text became a sort of "basic program" for France throughout the blockade of Beirut, and in the absence of any equally well-defined policy among the other members of the EEC (with the exception of Greece), France attempted to have it adopted by the entire Community.

The European Council of Brussels (28–29 June 1982)[168]

Following Mitterand's declaration the Israeli government, partially supported by the Americans, made every effort to prevent the French propositions from being ratified by the Ten and by the Security Council. The United States vetoed the French-inspired resolution at the United Nations. Israel accused France of "flying to the assistance of the PLO" and a spokesman of the minister of foreign affairs in Jerusalem cast doubt upon the possibility of including France (and the other European states, if they supported her) in a multinational force in Beirut. On the other side, Paris and the PLO campaigned for the endorsement of the French position by the EEC: Arafat made an appeal to the Europeans as did Druse leader Walid Jumblatt, whose organization was then in close contact with the French government. Saudi Arabia also supported the French proposals and Egyptian President Mubarak sent a message to the same effect to the Ten during the European Council.

The European summit conference at Brussels met in a general climate of dissatisfaction with the United States. The American role during the Lebanese crisis was merely one reason for that mood. As crucial a factor was the economic and commercial "guerilla warfare" waged against Europe by Washington, including "violations" of the summit agreement at Versailles, taxes on the importation of European steel, the technological embargo on European companies who traded with the USSR, high American interest rates and the rise in the exchange rate of the dollar.

In discussions on the Near East, the Ten found themselves confronting Paris' proposals as well as the question of possible sanctions demanded by Athens. There was clear opposition to "severe" economic sanctions which would have included suspending the 1975 agreement or boycotting Israeli exports. Contrary to the Greek demand and contrary to their reactions to the Falklands crisis, the imposition of martial law in Poland, or the seizure of hostages in Teheran, the Ten limited themselves to two rather symbolic acts. On the one hand, they put off indefinitely signing the second financial-aid agreement with Israel (48 million ECU = approx. $40 million), a postponement which had already been decided on 14 June, and they refused to convene the EEC-Israel Council of Cooperation, created by the agreement of 1975, which was to have met in July 1982. On the other hand, without an official collective decision of the EEC the Ten decided, individually, to place an embargo on military shipments to Israel.[169] But these shipments consisted only of individual items and were of minimal importance.

It does not seem, however, that France would have supported the harsh position taken by Athens with regard to possible sanction. Mitterand did not believe that such sanctions would be very effective and thought they would only cause increased Israeli inflexibility.

Although Mitterand said after the summit that the declaration which was adopted responded to his preoccupations, an attentive comparison of the 29 June declaration of the Ten on the Middle East with Mitterand's declaration of 24 June shows that the French president only partially convinced his partners. Here is the text adopted by the European Council, which was only settled upon after long and painful discussions involving a particularly brutal confrontation between Prime Ministers Schmidt and Papandreou:

> 1. The Ten maintain their vigorous condemnation of the Israeli invasion of Lebanon. They are greatly concerned about the situation in that country

and in particular in Beirut. They believe that the present ceasefire must at all costs be preserved.

The ceasefire should be accompanied on one hand by an immediate withdrawal of Israeli forces from their positions around the Lebanese capital as a first step towards their complete withdrawal, and on the other hand by a simultaneous withdrawal of the Palestinian forces in West Beirut in accordance with procedures to be agreed between the parties.

In order to facilitate this withdrawal the separation of forces would be controlled during this short transition period by Lebanese forces and, by agreement with the Lebanese government, by U.N. observers or forces.

2. The establishment of a final peace in Lebanon requires the complete and prompt withdrawal of Israeli forces from that country as well as the departure of all foreign forces except those which may be authorised by a legitimate and broadly representative government of Lebanon whose authority would be fully reestablished over all its national territory. The Ten support all efforts for the achievement of these objectives.

3. For the present the Ten have decided to continue their activity to bring relief to the population in distress and in this context, call on all parties to act in accordance with Security Council resolution 511 and 512 and to cooperate with the responsible international agencies as well as with UNIFIL. They are also ready in due course to assist in the reconstruction of the country.

4. Anxious to initiate, over and above the settlement of the Lebanese problem, the lasting restoration of peace and security in the region, the Ten wish to see negotiations based on the principles of security for all states and justice for all peoples. All the parties concerned should be associated with these and thus should accept one another's existence. Israel will not obtain the security to which it has a right by using force and creating "faits accomplis" but it can find this security by satisfying the legitimate aspirations of the Palestinian people, who should have the opportunity to exercise their right to self-determination with all that this implies.

They believe that for negotiations to be possible the Palestinian people must be able to commit themselves to them and thus to be represented at them. The position of the Ten remains that the PLO should be associated with the negotiations.

The Ten wish to see the Palestinian people in a position to pursue their demands by political means and wish that the achievement of these should take account of the need to recognise and respect the existence and security of all.

Condemnation of the invasion and the demand for Israel's total withdrawal from Lebanon were not new elements; they had already appeared in the appeal of the ministers of foreign affairs of 10 June. Only the appeal for the disengagement of forces around Beirut and the offer of European cooperation with the UN remained from Mitterand's original declaration. By contrast, all the parties (and not only Israel) were called upon to respect the cease-fire, and the demand for the retreat of the PLO forces was mentioned without repeating the French demand for an "honorable retreat" of the PLO.

In contrast to the French declaration, the appeal of the Ten insisted on the departure of *all* foreign forces. And, above all, the appeal for the neutralization of West Beirut, which was the central point of Mitterand's declaration, was not reiterated. In fact, the only relative "victory" of the camp which sought to accord a major role to the PLO lay in recalling the "great" principle of Venice: that the PLO (even after its defeat and evacuation) *must* be associated with the peace negotiations. The final declaration was a partial defeat for the countries (France, Greece, Ireland) which had hoped that a new stage might be reached in recognizing the PLO as a "necessary partner" and the right of the Palestinians "to choose the state structure of their choice." The reader of the Brussels declaration thus is left somewhat under the impression that while the PLO was besieged in Beirut, a simple replay of Venice had taken place.

In conclusion one can speak of the partial defeat of the pro-PLO camp and especially of France and, consequently, of a partial victory for the "moderates" (Germany, Denmark and Holland) in the first European Council after the Israeli offensive. *Le Quotidien de Paris* declared: "The reservations of the Europeans constitute, without doubt, a reversal for Mitterrand," and *Le Figaro* summarized: "The summit ended in what appears to be a failure of the French thesis on Lebanon." This general consensus on the results of the summit elicited several responses.

The Israeli reaction to the declaration of the Ten, although negative, was relatively moderate: "Developments within the region prove that Israel could not have acted otherwise in Lebanon. The Declaration of the Ten is contrary to the peace process."

The PLO's reaction was rather bitter. The PLO office in Brussels decried the absence of sanctions against Israel and the fact that the Council "had not been able once more to take a clear and straightforward decision in favor of an independent State for the Palestinians." The hopes of the Ten that "the Palestinian people might be in a position to pursue their demands *only* by political means indicates an alignment with Israeli-American positions," and "the European Council has placed the aggressor and the aggressee on the same footing," they lamented.

Finally, the timidity of the declaration pushed France to act alone in order to try to "save" the leadership of the PLO. That was the action taken by Paris against the background of silence from the other European capitals in July and August of 1982.

Toward the Evacuation of the PLO

The two months preceding the evacuation from Beirut were particularly marked by highly active French diplomatic efforts, in contrast with the passivity of the other members of the EEC. France had manifestly chosen two fundamental goals for itself. First, it sought to guarantee an "honorable" retreat from West Beirut for the PLO (and especially to prevent the organization's annihilation). In discussing the European multi-national force in Beirut, contrary to the Israeli government, which spoke of a "force to supervise the withdrawal of the PLO," Paris spoke only of an "interposed force," and thus emphasized that its deployment had to be approved by all parties, including the PLO. In addition, France attempted to tie the problem of West Beirut closely to the whole Palestinian problem and to take advantage of the emotions aroused by the blockade in order to persuade the Security Council to modify Resolution 242. Paris wished to have the "legitimate rights of the Palestinian people" recognized as well as the "right to self-determination," and "the necessity of mutual recognition between Israel and the PLO."

To achieve those ends the French government developed a large-scale diplomatic offensive. On the rhetorical level, from the beginning of July it propounded the thesis that the PLO had become "respectable" and had definitely renounced armed struggle in order to devote itself to political action. The French leaders repeated this theme constantly. They used, among others, the appeal of Pierre Mendes-France, Nahum Goldman and Philip Klutznick, Uri Avneri's interview of Arafat and, of course, but with some prudence, Arafat's signature on the McKloskey document,[170] in which the leader of the PLO affirmed that he accepted "all" the UN resolutions on the Palestinian problem. In his speech at the French Assemblée Nationale on 6 July Claude Cheysson declared: "As for the PLO, it has accepted the transition from the stage of armed struggle to the political stage. We have been assured of that. . . . The [Arafat document] confirms what France already knew, that the PLO is willing to move to the stage of political action."[171]

On the practical level, France increased its contacts with the leaders of the PLO, both in Beirut (the Gutmann-Delaye mission) and in Paris where, for the first time, the president of the Republic received Kaddumi officially (though as a member of the Arab League delegation):[172] But above all, one saw the formation of a true "Paris-Cairo axis" with Egypt and France coordinating their activities, especially at the UN.

These French initiatives were very poorly received in Israel. Relations between the two countries were shaken by President Mitterand's allusion to Oradour, a French town where the Germans had shot most of the inhabitants on 10 June 1944: "Military interventions, when they encounter resistance, always create Oradours. . . . I did not accept it in France, and I do not accept them in Lebanon," he proclaimed.[173] Relations were further strained by the massacre at the Jewish restaurant on the rue des Rosiers one month later, which gave the impression that Paris was more concerned with saving a terrorist organization than with fighting terrorism within France itself.[174]

In contrast, the PLO saw Paris as its only source of possible salvation, and could only regret that France and Athens had not succeeded in winning over the rest of their European partners. After having vigorously condemned the Israeli offensive the British fell silent. The Germans, the Dutch and the Danes were not convinced by the French arguments. Upon his return from a visit to the Near East as the official emissary of the EEC, German Foreign Minister Dietrich Genscher said that he had received the impression that "the moderate Arab countries would *not* appreciate an European initiative *cut off* from American policies." He continued, "We are naturally interested in being in harmony with our American friends, and working towards a joint position."[175]

The ministers of foreign affairs of the Ten, meeting on 19 July on political cooperation, were given a choice between two approaches: that of France, aimed at reinforcing the status of the PLO, and that of Germany, aimed at European-American coordination.[176] It was the second approach which gained the support of the majority of the countries of the EEC. Rather than take an independent initiative, they preferred to coordinate their actions with Washington and have the US exert pressure on Israel. Athens was not able to function as an effective ally for France within the European Council because of its extremism. Just as had occurred at the European Council, therefore, the French position was not adopted.

During August 1982 the Ten were confronted with three "hardline" resolutions proposed by the non-aligned countries and certain Eastern bloc countries during the extraordinary emergency session of the UN on Palestine. With the exception of Greece they all abstained. The official Community position was presented in the following fashion by Helskov, the Danish representative:

> The Ten reiterate their vigorous condemnation of the Israeli invasion of Lebanon, which constitutes a flagrant violation of international law and of the most elementary humanitarian principles. The Ten remain deeply committed to the restoration of the independence, sovereignty, territorial integrity and national unity of Lebanon which are indispensable for peace in the region.
>
> An urgent solution must be found to the tragic situation in Lebanon. At the same time, the problem of Lebanon cannot be seen in isolation,

but must be viewed in the broader context of the Middle East. The events which we are witnessing show again the crucial need for a comprehensive, just and lasting peace settlement in the Middle East that will meet the legitimate rights of the Palestinian people. The necessity thereof, in the view of the Ten, is well reflected in the French Egyptian draft resolution now before the Security Council.

Eager to initiate, over and above the settlement of the Lebanese problem, the lasting restoration of peace and security to the region, the Ten in their statement of 29 July 1982, in accordance with previous statements, notably the Venice Declaration, stressed once again their wish to see negotiations based on the principles of security for all states and justice for all peoples. All the parties concerned should be associated with those negotiations and thus should accept one another's existence. In the Ten's view, Israel will not obtain the security to which it has a right through the use of force and the creation of faits accomplis, but will find that security only by satisfying the legitimate aspirations of the Palestinian people, which should have the opportunity to exercise its right to self-determination, with all that this implies. The Ten believe that for negotiations to be possible the Palestinian people must be able to commit itself to them and thus to be represented at them. In this connection, the position of the Ten remains that the Palestinian Liberation Organization should be associated with the negotiations. The Ten wish to see the Palestinian people in a position to pursue its demands by political means and wish that the achievement of these demands would take account of the need to recognize and respect the existence and security of all.

The Ten are deeply concerned by the situation in Lebanon following the Israeli invasion. They are horrified by the loss of human life, by the intense suffering of the civilian population, and by the massive destruction resulting from the conflict. In particular, the situation in Beirut is intolerable. In their common statement on 26 June 1982 in this Assembly the Ten urged that that city be spared any further fighting. Instead, hostilities escalated, with heavy bombing and shelling of the densely populated areas of West Beirut and the infliction of further terrible suffering on the Lebanese and Palestinian populations. The Ten condemn the heavy bombardment of civilian areas in Beirut from land, sea and air, even after the PLO had made clear its decision to leave Beirut. They express particular concern at reports of civilian casualties caused by the use of phosphorous shells by Israeli forces. While stressing the total unacceptability of further attacks on West Beirut, the Ten note with satisfaction that the most recent cease-fire is holding.

The Ten urge Israel to respect the authority of the Security Council. They deeply regret its failure to do so. In the first place, Israel failed to comply with Security Council resolutions 508 (1982) and 509 (1982), including the demand for the withdrawal of all Israeli military forces forthwith and unconditionally to the internationally recognized boundaries of Lebanon. Despite the repeated demands of the Security Council for the cessation of military activities, there have been numerous and massive violations of the cease-fires which had been arranged. Israel has to date refused to accept the deployment of United Nations observers to monitor the situation in and around Beirut in defiance of decisions of the Security Council. It has also failed to comply with a call by the Security Council for the prompt return of Israeli troops to the lines they occupied on 1 August 1982. The blockade of the city of Beirut has not yet been lifted, despite repeated demands by the Security Council.

The Ten are shocked by recent reports on the consequences of that blockade and urge the Government of Israel to recognize its humanitarian responsibilities and permit unhindered access for supplies to meet the urgent needs of the civilian populations and allow the distribution of aid by United Nations agencies and non-governmental organizations. The Ten are also concerned about the future of the thousands of Palestinian prisoners held by Israel.

In their common statement of 29 June 1982 the Ten expressed the view that it was essential that the establishment of a lasting cease-fire in Beirut should be accompanied, on the one hand, by an immediate withdrawal of Israeli forces from their positions around the Lebanese capital as a first step towards their complete withdrawal and, on the other, by a simultaneous withdrawal of the Palestinian forces in West Beirut in accordance with procedures to be agreed upon between the parties. The Ten have followed closely the important efforts which have been under way for some time to bring about a peaceful outcome to the conflict in Beirut. They support such efforts and hope that they will lead to a solution which will spare the civilian population of the city further suffering.

In that common statement of 29 June 1982 the Ten also stressed that the establishment of final peace in Lebanon requires the complete and prompt withdrawal of Israeli forces from that country, as well as the departure of all foreign forces, except those which may be authorized by a legitimate and broadly representative Government of Lebanon whose authority would be fully re-established over all its national territory.

Deeply moved by the terrible suffering of the people of Lebanon and of the Palestinians living in that country, the members of the European Community have contributed, either directly or through the Community, to the urgent humanitarian relief operations being conducted in Lebanon. For the present, the Ten have decided to continue their activity to bring relief to the population in distress. They express their appreciation of the work being carried out by the different international agencies under the most difficult conditions. They call on all parties to act in accordance with the relevant Security Council resolutions, to permit the relief to reach all those in need of assistance without discrimination and to cooperate with the responsible international agencies, as well as with the United Nations Interim Force in Lebanon (UNIFIL). The Ten are also ready in due course to assist in the reconstruction of the country.

There must be an immediate end to the fighting in Lebanon. The Lebanese government must be enabled to reassert fully its authority over all its national territory. All Israeli military forces, along with all other foreign forces, must leave Lebanon in accordance with the wish of the Lebanese government. At the same time, a solution to the Lebanese problem should be accompanied by efforts towards establishing that dialogue between the parties which is so indispensable for achieving a solution to the Palestinian problem and a comprehensive peace in the Middle East.[177]

It is interesting to compare this statement with the separate explanations given by the French and Greek representatives to the UN.

The French representative, M. Louet, justified his country's abstention as follows:

The French delegation regrets that it was not able to vote for the three resolutions.

With regard to resolution A/ES-7/L.5, many of its paragraphs meet with our agreement, but several formulations could not be accepted—in particular, those which tended to impinge upon the competence of the Security Council. Moreover, that resolution in particular does not seem to us timely under present conditions. Although my delegation was not opposed in principle to the idea of the international conference referred to in resolution A/E5-7/L.6, we feel that the elements of a settlement must be found through a discussion among the existing states and political forces in the region, including the Palestinians, which implies the presence of the PLO in the negotiations. If after such a process a chance of success should arise, an international conference could then be useful, but at the present stage the idea seems premature.

However, that to us is not the principal problem: the essential point, in our view, is to restore peace to Lebanon—particularly to Beirut, a city whose unmitigated suffering has shocked us, as indeed we have also been shocked by the numerous tragic deaths of innocent, helpless unarmed civilians who were facing overwhelming violence.

Moreover, priority must be given to the efforts currently under way to promote a solution to the problem of Beirut. The humanitarian problems must be solved in the immediate future, be it a matter of aid to the victims or protection of the inhabitants of Beirut. It is also necessary to ensure the departure of the Palestinian fighters in conditions of security and dignity. All those elements are inextricably linked.

Basically, France's position on the essential issues is well known: it has many times condemned Israel's acts of aggression and has reaffirmed that Lebanon, a friendly country, must recover independence, territorial integrity and national sovereignty—which means the departure of all foreign forces from Lebanon.

In this spirit it is important in our opinion to respect Security Coucil resolutions and to apply the three principles recently recalled to us by the President of the French Republic: the right of the people of Israel to live in peace within the secure borders of a state that is recognized and respected by all; the right of the Palestinian people to have a homeland and to set up therein institutions of its choice; the right of the Lebanese people to regain its unity and independence which are flouted today.

After long and painful weeks we can finally see for Beirut the hope of a solution accepted by all the parties concerned.

Once that step has been taken, it will be necessary to focus our efforts on the political aspects of the present crisis. That is the purpose of the draft resolution introduced by France and Egypt in the Security Council. Both of our countries feel that it is still timely.[178]

Greece, which had been organizing public demonstrations against Israel since June, voted enthusiastically for the three UN resolutions, and its representative, Mr. Ghikas, explained his vote in the following way:

My delegation wishes to associate itself fully with the statements made to this Assembly on behalf of the 10 member countries of the European Community by the representative of Denmark in his capacity as Chairman ad interim of the Ten. However, I do feel the need to express, as well, how deeply the people and government of Greece have been shocked by the extent of the material damage and, even more, by the great number of victims which the Israeli invasion of Lebanon continues to cause, both among the Lebanese civilian population and among the Palestinian civilians who have taken refuge in that country.

The Greek government has unequivocably condemned this invasion, as well as Israel's obstinate refusal to comply with the repeated decisions of the Security Council calling upon it to put an end to its aggression and immediately and unconditionally to withdraw its troops from Lebanon. This refusal on Israel's part constitutes a further flagrant violation of the Charter of the United Nations, Article 25 of which expressly provides that: "The Members of the United Nations agree to accept and carry out the decisions of the Security Council. . . ." This same refusal has also taken the form of constant violations of cease-fires declared by the Security Council in the Beirut area.

In these conditions it is reassuring at least to note that the tenacious efforts exerted over long weeks to spare the population of Beirut new and further sufferings are finally moving towards a successful conclusion, despite the particularly lethal bombings of recent days which seemed close to destroying those efforts. Let me recall, in this regard, that, desirous of contributing to the restoration of peace, the Greek government declared itself willing to participate in the multinational force which, under such an agreement, could be dispatched to Lebanon.

If, as we hope, such an agreement is concluded, a first and far from negligible step will have been taken towards restoring peace in Lebanon— a peace which, in conformity with the desires of Lebanon's inhabitants and its government, could serve to ensure the unity, sovereignty and territorial integrity of that country.

A lasting peace, however, cannot be achieved so long as a just solution has not been found to the Palestinian question. Present events, which are nothing but a particularly tragic repercussion of the Palestinian problem, give further and irrefutable proof of that. It is thus necessary and urgent, parallel with the restoration of peace in Lebanon, to redouble efforts towards a speedy, comprehensive solution to the Palestinian problem.

The position of the Greek government in this regard is clear and well known: the solution of the Palestinian problem lies in recognition of the legitimate rights of the Palestinian people, including its right to self-determination and, thus, to the establishment of its own independent and sovereign state, as well as in the right of all states of the region to live in peace within secure and recognized boundaries.

The Greek government also feels that the process leading to such a solution can be begun in earnest only with the direct participation of the Palestine Liberation Organization, the sole, legitimate representative of the Palestinian people. Only if that condition is met can all the parties concerned enter into a dialogue capable of leading to a settlement of this conflict which has already taken too great a toll and whose continuation, by threatening peace and stability in the Middle East, poses a very grave and permanent threat to world peace.[179]

The "leading" position taken by France and Greece, in contrast with the other eight members of the EEC, was demonstrated rather symbolically by the meeting held that the PLO leaders were evacuated from Beirut (although the French President did not wish to meet the head of the PLO at that point). Mitterand declared at Athens: "France and Greece have contributed to the appeasement in the Near East, by holding in common to the idea that nothing will be possible unless the rights recognized by international society are acknowledged for the peoples and states of that region. . . . Greece is a remarkable asset in the necessary steps [towards pacification] even if there is no identity in our daily diplomatic efforts."[180]

The Europeans, the Reagan Plan and Fez

Sabra and Shatilla

After the PLO's evacuation from Beirut the problematic nature of the Lebanese crisis changed. With the exception of small skirmishes, combat died down. The themes upon which the Europeans had concentrated—disengagement of forces, the bombardments, the exit of the PLO—ceased to be of immediate importance. The PLO quickly reconstituted part of its forces beneath the Syrian umbrella. From the European point of view, the situation dropped from the emergency level to the routine of normal diplomatic procedures. However, the Reagan plan proposed immediately after the evacuation of Beirut and the Fez summit, one week later, provided the Ten with the ingredients for a new diplomatic offensive.

There was, of course, the last urgent crisis connected with the Israeli presence in Beirut: Sabra and Shatilla. European public opinion was severely shocked by the massacres and the European mass media were particularly unrestrained in attacking Israel. The impact of the massacres led even the most moderate governments of the EEC (Germany, Holland, Denmark and Luxemburg) to harden their attitudes towards Israel. But the interest taken in the massacres was ultimately transitory. The Commission of Inquiry established in Israel did a great deal to rehabilitate Israeli democracy, if not the Begin government, in Europe. The declaration of the Ten on the massacres merits quotation:

> The Ten express their profound shock and revulsion at the massacre of Palestinian civilians in Beirut. They strongly condemn this criminal act and call for the necessary measures to be taken to ensure the safety of the civilian population. They welcome UN Security Council Resolution 521 and are ready to support, up to the limit of their capabilities, appropriate additional steps, including the strengthening of the UN observers team in Beirut and the possible deployment of UN or multinational forces.
>
> They strongly deplore the violation of the Habib plan and demand the immediate withdrawal of the Israeli forces from West Beirut. They are convinced that the interests of Lebanon and of the region require the earliest possible withdrawal of all foreign forces except those authorized by the government of Lebanon, whose authority should be fully reestablished over all its national territory.
>
> The member states of the European Community remain greatly concerned about the situation in Lebanon as a whole. They strongly condemn the assassination of the president-elect of Lebanon. They appeal to all parties to show moderation and prevent further violence in that country.
>
> The Ten reaffirm their solidarity with a friendly country whose population has suffered so cruelly and whose fragile stability is dangerously threatened. They are confident that the Lebanese people will be able to elect a new president in accordance with their constitution and to bring about national reconciliation. They renew their offer to assist in the relief and reconstruction of the country.
>
> The tragic events in Lebanon have once again demonstrated that the Middle East can enjoy true peace and lasting stability only through a comprehensive settlement to be concluded with the participation of all parties, which

means that the PLO will have to be associated with negotiations. Such a settlement should be based on the principles of security for all states in the region, including Israel's right to exist, justice for all people, including the right of self-determination for the Palestinians with all that this implies, and mutual recognition by all the parties involved.

We must note that, contrary to the desire of four foreign ministers (Pym, Cheysson, Haralambopoulos and Colombo), Israel was not *explicitly* accused of the massacres. Its indirect responsibility can only be read between the lines of the declaration which appears to establish a link between the massacres, the violation of the Habib plan and the demand for Israeli withdrawal from West Beirut.[181]

The Diplomatic Offensive Around the Reagan Plan

Apart from the massacres at Sabra and Shatilla, President Reagan's announcement of his peace plan and the Fez summit dominated the Europeans' efforts during the fall of 1982 and the following winter. The American president's declaration, made on 1 September 1982, showed movement towards the European position, although it still remained quite distant from it. The convergence of American and European views was expressed on two levels.[182] First, Reagan insisted on the "legitimate rights of the Palestinians," and on the fact that the military losses of the PLO had not diminished the aspiration of the Palestinian people for a just solution to their problem. Even though that formulation was rather vague, it was the first time the Americans had presented the rights of the Palestinians as a central issue. In addition, Reagan, like the Europeans, criticized Israel sharply, warning her that military superiority alone could not bring a just and durable peace, and notified her that the United States opposed any new settlements on the West Bank and the Gaza Strip. Like the Europeans, Reagan insisted on his opposition to all annexation or permanent Israeli control over the West Bank and the Gaza Strip, and warned Israel that it understood Resolution 242 as "applying to all fronts."

From another point of view, important differences separated the Reagan plan and the Venice Declaration. They turned particularly upon two fundamental points of the latter text: Reagan avoided evoking a possible role for the PLO in negotiations, and he did not speak of "self-determination" but rather of "self-government of the Palestinians of the West Bank" in association with Jordan.

Despite the differences, the Reagan plan was very well received in Europe, especially by the more "moderate" governments, which favored cooperation with the United States and were relatively pro-Israeli. As the *Financial Times* put it: "With Reagan now moving some way towards the ideas contained in the EEC Venice Declaration on the Middle East, the possibility of a wider consensus might begin to emerge."[183] And according to the *Guardian:* "It would be useful if Europe and the U.S. would work together. The U.S. had, after all, come a long way since Europe adopted the Venice Declaration, and there is enough in the Reagan package to compensate for what is missing, including a specific role for the PLO."[184]

Even a country as mistrustful of American initiatives as France regarded Reagan's remarks positively. Immediately after their publication, Mitterand declared: "The spirit which inspired the Franco-Egyptian text [submitted to the Security Council] continues to be our own. Ronald Reagan's position seems to be oriented in the direction we had defined."[185] Three months later, however, the French President showed a bit more reserve: "[The Franco-Egyptian proposal] has an approach with a tighter hold on the reality of that part of the world [the Middle East] than the Reagan Plan, but Paris and Cairo wished to give the latter a chance, having considered it as a first stage."

The second event of the beginning of September 1982 was the Arab summit at Fez, which published a "Final Declaration." This text represented an extensively revised version of the Fahd plan, which the Arab heads of state had rejected at their previous meeting, and it seemed to concretize the victory of the so-called moderates, to whom the American president had addressed his plan.[186] The two points which pleased the Europeans were the recognition of all the states of the Middle East (seen by some as an *implicit* recognition of Israel) and the appeal for the departure of *all* foreign forces·from Lebanon (apparently including the Syrians). Yasser Arafat, who had endorsed that declaration, did a great deal to emphasize its value, particularly while he was present at the session of the Parliamentary Union in Rome.[187]

The Europeans greeted the text of the Fez Declaration favorably, although with some reservations. For example, the Germans thought it nebulous. But everyone saw a certain flexibility in it, which deserved encouragement. The Ten then issued a resolution calling for the implementation of the Reagan plan as a first step towards a global solution, and emphasized the "Spirit of Fez.":

[The Ten] welcome the new American initiative contained in President Reagan's speech on 1 September 1982. In the view of the Ten it offers an important opportunity for peaceful progresson on the Palestinian question and a step towards the reconciliation of the parties' conflicting aspirations.

The Ten appeal to all parties to seize the present opportunity to initiate a process of mutual rapprochement leading towards a comprehensive peace settlement.

In this connection they underline the importance of the statement adopted by Arab heads of state and government at Fez on 9 September, which they see as an expression of the unanimous will of the participants, including the PLO, to work for the achievement of a just peace in the Middle East encompassing all states in the area, including Israel.

They call now for a similar expression of a will to peace on the part of Israel.

They believe that discussions of the Franco-Egyptian draft resolution by the Security Council could play a useful part in establishing a common basis for a solution of the problems of the area.

It should be noted that the declaration of 20 September constituted an important change: from then on the Europeans based their common policy on the Reagan plan, Fez and the Franco-Egyptian proposals, whereas the Venice Declaration was *relegated to the background.* That was the first time since 1980 that its principles were not explicitly mentioned.

During the last months of 1982 the Europeans increased their contacts both with the PLO and with Israel in an attempt to influence them to accept the Reagan plan. The members of the EC sought to convince the PLO to declare that it had renounced armed struggle and to convince Israel to freeze its settlement policy. That course of action was articulated in the speech given by the Danish minister Uffe Ullemann-Jensen in the name of the Ten at the UN General Assembly;[188] it was also implicit in these remarks of Belgian Foreign Minister Tindemans: "We must wait a while to see the direction in which the PLO will evolve. If it becomes a purely political organization and if the moderate remarks made by Mr. Arafat at Fez are confirmed, then the PLO will become the most important spokesman of the Palestinian people."[189] That was also the impetus for the meeting between the Danish minister and Kaddumi in New York ("The Ten are prepared to respond in a constructive manner to an eventual political initiative by the PLO")[190] and of the encounter between Claude Cheysson and Arafat on October 13, while the Palestinian leader was involved in negotiations with King Hussein on the procedures to be followed in response to the American plan.[191] At the end of November a stormy confrontation took place between the Danish minister of foreign affairs and the Israeli leaders in Jerusalem.[192]

Finally, the text adopted by the leaders of the governments of the Ten at Copenhagen (the European Council of 3–4 December) reaffirmed the interest of the Europeans in the Reagan plan and the Fez Declaration:[193]

The Situation in the Middle East, Including Lebanon

Following a report by the Presidency on recent contacts the European Council discussed events in the Middle East where two aspects in particular continue to cause deep concern.

First, as regards the Arab-Israeli conflict, the European Council expressed its disappointment at the delay in grasping the political opportunity created by the initiative contained in President Reagan's speech on 1 September 1982, and the will to peace expressed in the declaration of Arab Heads of State meeting at Fez on 9 September 1982.

It called upon each of the parties to assume its international responsibilities without further hesitations. It expects each of the parties to cease to ignore the United Nations Security Council resolutions and explicitly make known their approval of these resolutions.

Secondly, the European Council continued to view the situation in Lebanon with the greatest concern. It particularly noted that in spite of the various efforts made by the negotiators on the spot, no significant progress had yet been achieved towards the withdrawal of the Israeli, Syrian, and other foreign forces.

The persistence of this situation would constitute a threat to the integrity and unity of Lebanon, carrying serious dangers for the whole region.

The withdrawal of foreign forces could be of a progressive nature, but should take place within a fixed and short period of time and under conditions which would permit the Lebanese authorities to exercise fully their rights of sovereignty over all of Lebanon.

The Ten have already demonstrated their willingness to contribute to the solution of the problems, especially by giving their support to the UN forces and UN observers established by the Security Council as well as the multi-national force in Beirut to which two of their number contribute. The Ten and the Community are equally prepared to continue to contribute to the reconstruction of Lebanon.

The Negative Reaction of the Interested Parties and the Return of the Ten to a "Low Profile" and a Flexible Attitude

The Europeans, like the Americans, were obliged to note that the Reagan plan was rejected by two of the three parties to whom it was addressed: Israel and the PLO. Only the so-called moderate Arab states had approved it.

The first negative reaction to the Reagan plan was that of the Israeli government (although the opposition leader, Shimon Peres, said that he accepted seventy percent of it). The Reagan plan clashed with the basic principles of the Begin government on the very points where it was closest to the Venice Declaration. In general the Israeli position was hostile to any change or addition to Camp David. In the case of the declarations of the Europeans, moreover, Jerusalem was irritated by the constant reference made by the Ten to the "spirit of Fez." We shall quote on characteristic reaction, that of the Minister of Foreign Affairs, Yitzhak Shamir: "We are not satisfied with the European attitude with regard to problems which we must confront. . . . the European declarations . . . contribute nothing to peace and stability in the region."[194] In February 1983 Shamir went on a tour of the European capitals to explain the Israeli rejection of the American and European plans and to ask that, despite that rejection, the Ten lift the "sanctions" imposed in June 1982.[195]

The reactions of the PLO were also negative, but the deep internal struggle that developed within that organization between Arafat and the more obdurate groups is well known. The Palestinian National Council meeting at Algiers in February 1983 did not formally renounce the Reagan plan as the Central Council of the PLO had done in Damascus in November 1982, but it judged it "insufficient." The stance was in fact, tantamount to rejection, because the Reagan speech represented a package deal. By contrast, the PNC at Algiers proclaimed its enthusiastic support for the Brezhnev plan of 1981. Another sign of the victory of the extremist camp was that Issam Sartawi was not authorized to speak at Algiers.[196]

It should be noted that the PLO and several of the Arab states did not look kindly upon Europe for seemingly abandoning all reference to the Venice Declaration, and for simply rallying around the American plan. In October 1982 the PLO delegate in Luxemburg, El Astal, deplored "the over-timid attitude of the EEC" and the fact that "the EEC had not adopted a policy more independent of the United States."[197] This constituted, in their view, an independent, distinct and even contrary policy to that of the United States,

The declaration on the Middle East adopted by the Ten at the European Council of Brussels (21–22 March 1983) represented yet another attempt to convince the PLO to take a more moderate line, and to encourage Arafat to come to an agreement with King Hussein. For that reason the Ten tried to present the Palestine National Council meeting in Algiers as a rather positive development. After all, the PNC had not explicitly rejected the Reagan plan *in toto*, and the Fez declaration was endorsed again—although half-heartedly—at Algiers. The Europeans also recalled that the Brezhnev plan, around which the PLO had rallied, recognized the right of all the states in the region, including Israel, to live in peace. They therefore chose to mention the PNC in their text, presenting its outcome in a positive light. Finally, in order to try once more to convince the PLO and influence the negotiations between Hussein and Arafat, they adopted a relatively "hard" tone against the Israeli settlements.[198]

> The Ten are deeply disturbed by the continued lack of progress towards peace between Israel and her Arab neighbors. They are convinced that all parties must seize the present opportunity to achieve the two most urgent objectives: the withdrawal of all foreign forces from Lebanon and a resumption of negotiations aimed at a comprehensive peace settlement.
>
> The Ten reaffirm their support for the sovereign and independent state of Lebanon and for its government, which should urgently be enabled to re-establish without restrictions its authority over the whole of its territory. This requires the prompt withdrawal of Israeli, Syrian and PLO forces. The Ten support the efforts of the United States to achieve this objective. They call on all concerned to conclude negotiations without further delay. They continue to support the peacekeeping role of UN and multinational forces in Lebanon.
>
> The principles which underlie the Ten's approach to wider peace negotiations, as set out in more than one previous statement, remain valid. A lasting peace can only be built on the right to a secure existence for all states in the region including Israel, and justice for all the peoples, including the right of the Palestinian people to self-determination with all that this implies. These rights must be mutually recognized by the parties themselves. Negotiations will have to embrace all the parties concerned including the Palestinian people; and the PLO will have to be associated with them. The threat or use of force must be renounced by all.
>
> President Reagan's initiative of 1 September 1982 indicated a way to peace, and the Arab summit meeting at Fez demonstrated a readiness for it. The task now is to move beyond statements of principle and find a means to reconcile and implement the various peace proposals. The conclusions of the recent meeting of the Palestine National Council can and should contribute to the peace process. The Ten therefore welcome the discussions between Jordan and the PLO. The Palestinian people and the PLO should seize the present opportunity by declaring themselves in favor of peace negotiations. This would be a major step forward, to which the Ten would expect all concerned to respond constructively.
>
> The Ten look to the Arab states to play their part by supporting those who seek a solution to the demands of the Palestinian people by political means.
>
> The efforts of the US will continue to be indispensable to create the conditions in which negotiations can begin.
>
> Above all the time has come for Israel to show that it stands ready for genuine negotiations on the basis of Security Council Resolutions 242

and 338, in the first place by refraining from enlarging existing settlements or creating new ones. These settlements are contrary to international law and a major and growing obstacle to peace efforts.

The Middle East is a region with which the Ten have long been closely associated and in whose future they have a deep interest. They intend to maintain their contacts with all the parties and to use their influence to encourage movement towards compromise and negotiatied solutions. They believe that this is in the best interest of the countries and the peoples of the region, of the Ten themselves and of their mutual relations.

The Ten express once again their growing concern at the continued conflict between Iraq and Iran, which constitutes an even more serious threat to the security and stability of the entire region.

The Ten deeply regret that none of the peace initiatives organized hitherto has succeeded in bringing the fighting to an end. They call for a cease-fire, the cessation of all military operations and the withdrawal of forces to internationally recognised frontiers; and for a just and honourable settlement negotiated in accordance with the resolutions of the UN Security Council and acceptable to both parties.

European reactions to the text of the European Council were rather disillusioned. Alluding to the crisis connected with the British contribution to the budget of the EEC, the *Times* noted that when the Ten were not in agreement about anything, they tended to publish a new declaration about the Middle East. The newspaper quoted a diplomat connected with the drafting of the declaration who stated that it was "exhortatory rather than exciting."[199] According to *La Cite* the Middle East appeal of the Ten "contained nothing very new or scintillating" and was the only result of a lackluster summit conference.[200]

For their part, the Israelis rejected the declaration of the Ten, stating the "it had no relation to reality" and was "unbalanced and incomprehensible."[201] The offical Syrian newspaper *Al-Baas* accused the Europeans of "continuing to place the aggressor and the aggressee on the same equal footing" and thus effectively supporting Israel.[202]

The failure of the Hussein-Arafat negotiations and the refusal of the Jordanian king to be the only leader to follow upon the path of the Reagan plan sounded the death knell for the efforts of the Europeans which, since 1982, had been predicated on the transformation of the PLO into a "political partner."

That failure, in addition to the polarization of the Community because of its serious internal problems, the question of Britain, and the problem of including Spain and Portugal doubtlessly explains the relative self-effacement of the Ten on the political scene of the near East. Consequently the declaration of the European Council of Stuttgart (17–19 June 1983) on the Middle East was one of the shortest and least significant published by the EEC on that topic up to that point (it should be borne in mind that Stuttgart was dominated by the question of the British contribution to the EEC budget):

> The Heads of State and Government consider that the return of full sovereignty and final peace in Lebanon requires the complete and prompt withdrawal of foreign forces from its territory, except for those whose presence may be requested by the Lebanese government.
>
> They confirmed their full support for President Gemayel and his government in their determined action to re-establish their authority over the entire territory of Lebanon. In this respect, they consider that the signing of the Israel-Lebanon agreement constitutes a step which must be followed by others. They consider, however, that peace will not be able to become a reality unless the security and legitimate interests of the other states and peoples of the region are taken into account.
>
> They state their readiness to use all the means at their disposal to support the efforts undertaken by the parties in question so as to find a broader area of agreement.
>
> They remain convinced that a just, lasting and comprehensive peace in the Middle East can only be secured on the basis of the principles which they have stated many times in the past.
>
> They again voice their very serious concern at the distress of the Palestinian civilian population. They hope that the relevant international organizations will be allowed to assist this population without hindrance.

One should also note a relative increase in flexibility of the Europeans with regard to Israel, which was undoubtedly influenced by three factors: (1) the intransigence of the PLO and its refusal to commit itself exclusively to the political path; (2) the Lebanese-Israeli agreement which was viewed by the Europeans as a positive development in the absence of any other prospect, and which had been approved by the ministers of the EEC at their informal meeting of 14–15 May in Gymnich;[203] (3) the role played by the country which was serving as president of the Community in the first half of 1983, the Federal Republic of Germany, which had fought intensely for the establishment of better relations between the Community and Israel (especially after the formation of the Kohl government in May). Germany insisted upon, and obtained the cancellation of, the "sanctions" of June 1982.

Actually, the Ten decided at Stuttgart that after the Lebanese-Israeli agreement, there were no further obstacles to signing the second financial agreement between Israel and the EEC, or to convening the Council of

Cooperation. (It should be noted that Greece, which had opposed the removal of sanctions until then, abstained in Stuttgart, a sign that Athens, which was on the verge of assuming the presidency of the Community on 1 July, did not wish to appear too "biased"). For Israel the most important decision of the Ten was not the rather insignificant amount of financial aid but the ending of the boycott and the possibility of renewing contacts with the Community at the highest level. One should also note that the Stuttgart Declaration was the first text promulgated by the Ten in several years which contained no criticism of Israel at all, not even raising the question of the settlements in the territories. Without doubt the agreement with Lebanon, followed by the ending of sanctions against Israel, had created a new climate.

At the Stuttgart meeting of the European Council, the ten Heads of State and Government declared:

> [We] remain convinced that a just, lasting and comprehensive peace in the Middle East can only be secured on the basis of the principles which [we] have stated many times in the past.

During the two years that followed (June 1982–June 1985), the Ten did not deal directly with the Palestinian question. Rather, they extensively discussed the situation in Lebanon, and the humanitarian aspects of the strife between the various Lebanese forces and militias. It could be said that the European Community shifted its attention from the Israeli-Palestinian conflict to the question of the national integrity of Lebanon. They justified their new perspective at the meeting of ten ministers of foreign affairs in Athens, on 12 September 1983:

> The Ten appeal for an immediate cease-fire leading to the cessation of violence and pressure in Lebanon, and to national reconciliation. . . . They are convinced that the abnormal situation in Lebanon, so long as it continues, is a further obstacle to the achievement of a just and lasting settlement in the Middle East as a whole.

During these two years, which were, marked by serious tensions within the Community (the question of the British participation to the EEC budget, the problem of Spain's and Portugal's entries into the Common Market, etc.), discussions related to the Middle East conflict were rather scarce. No major declaration which included new elements was published in 1984–85. Instead, the Ten adhered to the principles of the Venice declaration.

The Europeans could only watch with dismay as the "opportunities" opened by the Fez summit and by the Reagan plan faded away. However, they saw a ray of hope in the new dialogue opened by the King of Jordan with the "moderate" wing of the PLO.

FOUR

European Foreign Policy and the Arab-Israeli Conflict: An Evaluation

A Framework for Evaluation

European policy towards the conflict, especially within the Framework for Political Cooperation, is something of a paradox. On the one hand, there is no area of foreign affairs to which the Ten have paid more attention and more vigorously attempted to achieve the objectives of political cooperation. As we have seen in the preceding chapters, the last fourteen years have seen a flurry of European statements, declarations and activity surrounding the conflict—virtually spanning the "life" of the Framework itself. In terms of output, at least in a verbal sense, European political cooperation seems to have scored a success in relation to the Middle East and its problems.

And yet, if we search for tangible results in all this activity a strong sense of doubt creeps in. Is the European "presence" in the area any stronger since the commencement of the Framework for Political Cooperation? Is a European "solution" to the conflict any more imminent? Has Europe made any "internal gains" from its political cooperation activity? Our intuitive reply to these and similar questions would be negative, indicating a failure of policy accentuated by the importance the issue has assumed on the agenda of the Framework for Political Cooperation.

A closer look at the historical-political sequence of events indicates a variegated evaluation: disappointing to those who dream of European integration, surprising, perhaps, to the skeptics. In order to delineate the line between failure and success we propose to return to the three categories of political cooperation activity to which we referred in the opening chapter: active policy, reactive policy and reflexive policy. The utility of these categories lies in the ability to define with greater precision the objectives of the Framework for Political Cooperation in the context of the conflict—or for that matter in any other area of activity—and hence to have a better yardstick by which to judge results.

In the context of the Arab-Israeli conflict the *active policy* would be associated with a positive European role in the evolution of the conflict, which would ultimately set the parties on the path towards a global peace settlement. A minimum active goal would be to become a necessary, even indispensable, intermediary among the three parties—Israel, the Arab countries and the Palestinians. This active role would be part of a European strategy, particularly favored by France (and resisted by the Federal Republic of Germany) of assuming an independent global position between the two super-powers.

By contrast, a *reactive policy* would be one which had as its objective the simple preservation of the European interest, however this may be defined, in the face of events in the Middle East. Conflict management would be left to the parties, the superpowers or the United Nations. Europe would simply try to cut any of its losses which might emanate from the region and to contain any conflict spillover.

Needless to say, underlying both active and reactive approaches would be the belief that joint action would better serve the defined goals than individual uncoordinated member-state action.

Finally, the *reflexive policy* would be one which would "utilize" the Arab-Israeli conflict for internal objectives. This could be the building-up of European confidence in exercising its newly established mechanisms for foreign policy coordination; it could also be the maintaining of some "integrational momentum" on the external level in order to compensate for lack of progress on the internal scene.

As we emphasized in the first chapter, these three categories are developed for analytical purposes. We do not of course suggest that European foreign policy was actually shaped in anything like this orderly "academic" fashion; it was, naturally, the result of complex national, European and international inputs. But the categories are helpful, in our view, precisely because of the chaotic nature of European foreign policy-making: they provide a means of organizing, understanding and evaluating.

In relation to all three dimensions, it would seem as if the members of the EEC were well-positioned for success for they had solid friendly relations with all parties to the conflict. Here the plurality of the partners could be considered a distinct advantage, because privileged lines of communications to the different parties were available through different member states. They had profound historical knowledge of the region—

it could be said with a measure of irony that the Europeans states were the founding fathers of the international dimension of the conflict. They had close economic relations, often decisive, with the various parties. And finally both the Arabs and the Israelis had a tradition of special cultural ties to western Europe.

Active, Reactive and Reflexive Policy in Action

In an earlier chapter we saw that it was possible to divide European policy towards the Arab-Israeli conflict within the Framework for Political Cooperation into three distinct phases: (1) the period from the establishment of European political cooperation up until the Yom Kippur War (1970–1973); (2) the period from the Yom Kippur War up to (but not including) the Venice Declaration (1973–1979); (3) the period from the Venice Declaration up to (and including) the Lebanon War and its aftermath (1980–). It would appear from our earlier analysis that in this context the categorization of active, reactive and reflexive policy objectives assumes an historical meaning.

The Reflexive Period: 1970–1973

In the first period the predominant objective of the Framework for Political Cooperation was reflexive. The Middle East was an instrument for flexing European muscles innocuously. The Framework had barely been launched and nothing very ambitious would be appropriate for initial action. We should remember that the Arab-Israeli conflict was at a plateau stage. The Arabs were still reeling from the 1967 defeat, and the Palestinian problem was only beginning to be perceived widely as more than "the refugee problem"—the nomenclature still used in UN Security Council Resolution 242. At face value, even the internal reflexive results of that period were rather limited. The Six produced the Schumann document of 1971 which we have examined above and which did not amount to much more than a collage of non-binding ideas, as the aftermath of the 1973 war was to prove. At the same time it was in this context that the Framework for Political Cooperation cut its teeth. Mechanisms were tried, structures experimented with and not insignificant experience gained. The very fact that a joint declaration was issued in the field of foreign policy, an event now taken for granted, was an important innovation. Crawling simply had to precede walking.

The Reactive Period: 1973–1979

Although we call this period the reactive period, we must emphasize that the categories are not mutually exclusive. As the Community moved into a "higher" and more ambitious phase of policy making, it acted on the basis of the existing infrastructures and executing a reactive policy it inevitably reinforced the reflexive ones. In our analysis, however, we will emphasize the reactive element.

As we saw, the principal events which conditioned this phase were the oil crisis in the wake of the October war and the subsequent economic upheaval. Initial European reaction was uncoordinated. Later Europe developed a policy which sought to secure its energy resources—effectively, if we are not to mince words, by ingratiating itself with the Arab countries. The European states issued a series of declarations which increasingly recognized Palestininan rights and launched the Euro-Arab dialogue. The tangible results of this policy were questionable: the Nine competed among themselves for long-term oil supply contracts which indirectly contributed to the enormous price hikes of that period, and the Euro-Arab dialogue effectively remained moribund. It is difficult, however, to assess what the situation would have been had this policy not been pursued. We can simply note at this stage that the objectives of the Framework for Political Cooperation were to secure European interests, not through direct influence on actual events in the Middle East, but by peripherally taking certain reactive measures.

The Active Phase: 1980–

It was in this period that Europe made its debut into the peace process. This was the period of the Venice Declaration and the "European solutions" to the conflict. Having played a very low-key role in the Camp David talks and virtually being forced into grudging participation in the Sinai peace-keeping force, at odds with the reactive policy, Europe now tried to launch its own policy. Once again, we should recall that the Venice period cannot be couched exclusively in active terms. The reflexive and reactive goals were also affected. But for the first time— with what measure of seriousness it is difficult to know—Europeans were staking a claim to a policy of their own.

The two prongs of the initiative—the Declaration which consolidated the European position toward the Palestinians, including the introduction of the PLO element, and the subsequent intended actions in the area— did not really have a *direct* impact on the actors. Indeed, all parties, and primarily the Israelis and the Palestinians, rejected the Declaration as being too much or not enough.

The period of the war in Lebanon and its aftermath can be considered part of this active phase. Declarations in the mold of Venice and even "mini-sanctions" were adopted vis-à-vis Israel, though the impact of these measures was questionable.

Evaluation

Evaluation of any public policy is classically problematic: it is difficult to construe *post-facto* the possible effects of other options, a problem magnified in relation to the Arab-Israeli conflict. Has the foreign policy of any western power met with great success in the region in the last 14 years? By what criteria? There is an additional and troublesome "if" problem in the context of the Framework for Political Cooperation: we have to ask whether the achievements of the Framework enhanced or detracted from the individual policy initiatives of the Six, Nine and Ten.

The Active Goals

In this context the failure is almost complete. Despite the various declarations, visits, participation in multinational forces and all the rest, the European vision—at least if taken at face value—has not had a visible impact on the conflict. America directly, and the Soviet Union indirectly, remain the key actors, with Venice and its aftermath not really producing a real European presence. How can this failure be explained? There were of course contingent historical factors: the 1980 American presidential election, the 1981 Israeli elections (during which period the Europeans would do nothing which might damage Labor's chances), the 1981 victory of Mitterand, the assassination of Sadat and the Falklands crisis which removed the most ambitious "activist" in that period—the United Kingdom.

But there were other, more fundamental, causes which went beyond the particular constellation of unfavorable events.

Causes of the Failure. The relative success of the Americans in playing a role in the Middle East is partly due to their pragmatism, to the discretion of their diplomacy, which is essentially carried out in the corridors of power, to their refusal to impose ready made and definitive solutions, and above all to their massive commitment, both financial and military. The Europeans behaved in precisely the opposite fashion.

First, their method has been declaratory: they publish (or allow to be divulged) a text (a declaration or working paper) which offers ready made solutions, instead of indicating the means of achieving solutions. Thus when they affirmed that the solution must be reached through the Palestinian self-determination and the participation of the PLO in negotiations, they were taking a position on the solution itself. (And since that solution was rejected by Israel, the declarations had no effect.)

The importance of semantics in those declarations is even more problematic: because they are the result of a compromise among six, nine, or ten (and soon perhaps twelve) governments instead of being the work of a single government, the wording reaches a high level of complexity. Thus the declaration of June 1977 says:

> In the establishment of a just and lasting peace account must be taken of the legitimate rights of the Palestinians. . . . The Nine affirmed their belief that a solution to the conflict in the Middle East will be possible only if the legitimate right of the Palestinian people to give effective expression of its national identity is translated into fact, which would take account the need for a homeland for the Palestinian people.

The Venice Declaration states:

> A just solution must finally be found to the Palestinian problem, which is not simply one of refugees. The Palestinian people, which is conscious of existing as such, must be placed in a position, by an appropriate process defined within the framework of the comprehensive peace settlement, to exercise fully its right to self-determination. The achievement of these objectives requires the involvement and support of all the parties concerned in the peace settlement which the Nine are endeavoring to promote in keeping with the principles formulated in the declaration referred to above. Those principles apply to all the parties concerned, and thus the Palestinian people, and to the PLO, which will have to be associated with the negotiations.

These texts are characterized by their lack of clarity and the absence of operational significance.

It is even more serious that those declarations received no follow-up and implied no real commitment. The most highly developed activity of the Europeans has proved to be the ritual visits to the Middle East by the Council of Ministers' presidents. The economic aid of the Common Market to the parties to the dispute has also been very limited. In terms of military engagement, the MFO and the Multinational Force in Beirut are not "European" interventions, arms sales have remained purely bilateral, and there is no "European force" capable of intervening or even impressing the parties.

Another aspect of the European declarations which sheds light on their inefficacy is their one-sidedness, which is expressed in two ways.

On the one hand, if one analyzes the texts of 1971, 1973, 1977 and 1980, one finds that rather specific and ever-increasing demands were made upon Israel: total withdrawal from the territories rescinding the annexation of East Jerusalem, and recognition of the legitimate rights of the Palestinians, first of their right to a homeland, then of self-determination and finally the participation of the PLO in negotiations. There was no parallel increase in the demands made upon the Arab states and the PLO. The Europeans merely voiced a rather vague demand for recognition of Israel, which was not even a condition for the participation of the PLO in the negotiations. Thus one finds nothing about effective guarantees, the demilitarization of the "Palestinian homeland," public renunciation of military action by the PLO, etc. There is thus a disproportion, a total lack of balance in those declarations. If Israel is an essential party to the conflict, any plan must contain a *minimum* basis, if not acceptable to the Begin or Shamir governments, at least acceptable to a considerable portion of Israeli public opinion and some of the political forces within Israel. The European plans have been rejected even by most of the dovish wing of the Labor opposition, including Mapam, because they do not provide that minimum basis.

The Israelis object to the European proposals for several reasons. First, the concept of self-determination appears to be the springboard for a Palestinian state between Israel and Jordan, but since this is never openly mentioned there is also a failure to deal both with the problems which a state might create and possible solutions to such a problem; in addition, PLO participation is required without demanding *prior* recognition of Israel and the renunciation of all military action. Among the political parties in Israel today, the European plans are acceptable only to the *Progressive List for Peace, Rakah*, and perhaps *Ratz*, which form too narrow a base to assure their success.

Divergent European Attitudes Toward the United States. The positions taken by the Europeans with regard to American policy have been highly diverse. Today, for example, the Ten fall into four groups: (1) some remain rather inclined to line up with American foreign policy; (2) the majority desire an autonomous European foreign policy, but one which is coordinated with, and certainly not antagonistic to, American policy; (3) France desires a totally independent European policy; (4) and Papandreou's Greece has adopted a staunch anti-American policy. For that reason, reactions to pressure from Washington have been very divergent. Since 1973 it has been evident that the United States does *not* desire independent European initiatives in the Middle East.

The clearest demonstration of a split in Europe in response to American pressure occurred during the months following the Venice Declaration (November 1980–May 1981) when the Thatcher government deliberately thwarted the European initiative, in acquiescence to the wishes of the new American administration. These divergent attitudes towards Washington go far in explaining the lack of continuity and the ineffectiveness of European policies in the Middle East.

Deep Disagreement Concerning the Solution of the Palestinian Problem and the PLO. The "joint declarations" conceal rather poorly the absence of a consensus on the best way to solve the Palestinan problem and, above all, on the role to be accorded the PLO. Some countries, such as Holland, Luxemburg and Denmark, accepted the mention of the PLO in the Venice Declaration rather unwillingly, as "the best of bad alternatives." Others (England, Germany, and Belgium) viewed that reference as a necessary one but, for the moment, preferred it to remain just that—a reference. In contrast, France and Ireland sought to have the "right to self-determination" defined as the right *to a state* alongside Israel, and they wished to emphasize the necessary role of the PLO even further. Finally, Greece was completely identified with the Palestinian struggle and wanted the PLO to be recognized as the sole legitimate representative of the Palestinian people. Those differences of opinion were expressed particularly in the votes cast by the Europeans at the United Nations on questions concerning the Palestinians. In such a climate of serious differences of opinion, "declarations" cannot be taken seriously.

The Increasingly Serious Internal Crisis of the EEC. Since its creation the EEC has weathered a series of crises. During de Gaulle's time the great crisis of 1965 nearly put an end to the Common Market. Since its "relaunching" at the Hague in December 1969 the community has stumbled from crisis to crisis. The petroleum problem and the economic recession have had negative effects on the cohesion of its members. The inclusion of two countries which were very hesitant about European unity, the United Kingdom and Greece, also has had devastating effects: those countries have periodically questioned their further participation in the Community, have refused to make normal contributions to the Community budget, have challenged the common agricultural policy (of which France is the principal beneficiary) and so forth. 1983, a particularly negative year, was marked by two crisis summit conferences: Stuttgart (in June) and Athens (in December). Both meetings of the "European Council" (Heads of State and Government) were clouded by a very stormy atmosphere and by differences among the European leaders. Above all, there was complete disagreement on the question of the financial contribution of Great Britain to the budget of the Community.

In this atmosphere of discord on crucial internal problems, the grandiloquent declarations of the Europeans on any international crisis, be it the Falklands, Poland, Afghanistan or the Arab-Israeli conflict, can hardly have any impact. It would seem that each time a European summit conference ends with failure concerning internal issues, the participants feel the need to publish a new text on the Middle East, as if to give the impression of having achieved some sort of result.

If one has to find any real impact in the active sense of European policy, it could be speculated that Europe has helped to centralize the Palestinians as a key factor in the conflict and to legitimize, to a certain extent, approaches which would be more explicit in dealing with the problem than Camp David. It is not impossible that the road to the Reagan plan—so bitterly rejected by the Begin-Shamir government, and only tactically accepted by the Israeli Labor party—has gone through the Venice Declaration.

Reactive and Reflexive Goals

Whereas our assessment of the active dimension in impact terms is rather negative, it is more difficult to assess the other dimensions of the policy. If we return for one moment to our temporal analysis, it is clear that in the reflexive period nothing of substance was achieved, that in the reactive period the gains were probably mostly reflexive and that in the more recent active phase, the European gains are mostly reactive.

This "policy lag" gives us a clue to a reassessment of the European policy gains. In particular we would mention the following considerations. During the period under consideration Europe was able to keep itself almost totally out of direct conflicts with the protagonists in the conflict. The declarations undoubtedly had an appeasing effect on the Arabs, even if not as much as Europe had hoped, but nothing changed in the substantive policy towards Israel—including participation in the Sinai Multinational Force. In other words, if we move from the surface meaning of the declarations, and construe the last phase as overtly active—in response perhaps to increasing Arab pressure—but covertly reactive, the European policy could be considered more of a success than the initial analysis would suggest. The reaction to the war in Lebanon is symptomatic: first came the by-now usual declarations coupled with the fanfare of mini-sanctions, and then quietly everything returned to normal to the contentment of all parties. Whether this construction is a mere rationalization, an haphazard coincidence or in some sense premeditated, is a question we do not propose to answer.

The reactive-reflexive benefits may be evident in yet another way. It is clear that as a matter of *individual* member state foreign policy towards the conflict, in the wake of the 1973 war all the European partners were eager to shift their positions in favor of the Arab countries and the Palestinians. For countries like Denmark, Holland and above all the Federal Republic of Germany, this was potentially highly embarrassing vis-à-vis Israel. The Framework for Political Cooperation provided a mechanism through which this shift could take place with a minimum cost to the individual partners, each hiding behind the back of the others. Moreover, member states could and did argue that their presence within the Framework for Political Cooperation was an asset to the protagonists since things could be worse—depending on the party in question—

without the individual nation's input. Thus, for example, the Federal Republic could argue that it was exercising a moderating effect on France. This "shield effect" could also be utilitized in the internal national context to affect public opinion, legitimizing otherwise unacceptable action under the umbrella of European unity. In Italy, for example, the powerful Communist party could associate itself with a variety of policies—even if consonant with American interests—because the framework for action was political cooperation. The reverse of the "shield effect" would be the weakness inherent in Europe which presented a single focal point for external pressure. A successful declaration was an invitation for outside parties to ask other sides to participate.

If there were beneficiaries to the Framework for Political Cooperation they were probably not Europe in its collectivity but the individual member states who were able to manipulate the Framework as a shield for policy shifts.

In some ways this is very little to show for a political construct which set out to allow Europe to play its "proper role in the world." But then, has any other power fared significantly better from involvement in the Middle East than Europe, which has dialogued and traded at a profit with all parties to the Arab-Israeli conflict?

And yet there is a sense of profound disappointment that Europe, with its fledgling cooperation, has not been more successful.

Can western Europe play a collective role in the Arab-Israeli conflict? Given almost fifteen years of experience (1970–1983), it is rather difficult to answer affirmatively. At best one can attempt to formulate the conditions necessary for such a role.

1. Since a joint foreign policy is tied to the state of the Community, the EEC must *first* resolve its internal crises: no successful foreign policy has emerged from a power in internal disarray.
2. Before formulating common policy on the Middle East, the Ten must try to formulate a common policy with regard to the United States.
3. The Europeans must cease making solemn declarations and proposing ready-made solutions and, instead, use discreet diplomatic methods and suggest a range of possible methods for reaching a solution.
4. They ought to try to understand the protagonists better. This would probably entail sending separate missions to the various political forces in Israel, and to the different Palestinian factions (Arafat and Abu Mussa, the Palestinians in the territories, in the camps and in the diaspora) in order to determine what would and what would not be acceptable to them.

5. The Europeans should seek to harmonize their points of view on the Palestinian question and the future role of the PLO. What is "self-determination"? What does the participation of the PLO mean?

6. Any European initiative should maintain a certain proportion between the demands and criticisms leveled against Israel and those made of the Arab countries and the PLO, and not appear biased and unacceptable to one of the parties.

7. Finally, the Europeans must understand that their initiatives can never be effective if they do not commit themselves, if not militarily, then at least on the economic level. That implies massive aid to the various parties and the prospect of even more assistance if they accept European advice.

In recent years, the process of European integration within the European Community has been directed increasingly towards the formulation and execution of common policies in the foreign relations field. The emergence in the last decade of a Framework for Political Cooperation and massive growth in the external economic relations of the Community have been the most visible signs of this phenomenon.

Much of the effort of the ten member states of the European Community within the Framework of Political Cooperation has been devoted to the search for a meaningful role vis-à-vis the Middle East in general, and the Arab-Israeli conflict in particular. Efforts so far have concentrated on a series of declarations which, while showing at times a measure of internal cohesion, have not had a visible impact on events in that arena.

Simultaneously, the European Community, as part of its cooperation policy in the Mediterranean Basin, has concluded a series of Trade and Cooperation Agreements with several of the regional protagonists.

A feature of the European policy has been an almost total separation between these two facets of its Middle East posture.

A search for a more effective policy, important both to the Middle East countries and Europe itself continues.

Appendix

Solemn Declaration on European Union

Foreign Policy

In order to cope with the increasing problems of international politics, the necessary reinforcement of European Political Cooperation must be ensured, in particular by the following measures:

- intensified consultations with a view to permitting timely joint action on all major foreign policy questions of interest to the Ten as a whole;
- prior consultation with the other Member States in advance of the adoption of final positions on these questions. The Heads of State or Government underline their undertaking that each Member State will take full account of the positions of its partners and give due weight to the adoption and implementation of common European positions when working out national positions and taking national action;
- development and extension of the practice by which the views of the Ten are defined and consolidated in the form of common positions which then constitute a central point of reference for Member States' policies.
- progressive development and definition of common principles and objectives as well as the identification of common interests in order to strengthen the possibilities of joint action in the field of foreign policy;
- coordination of positions of Member States on the political and economic aspects of security;
- increased contacts with third countries in order to give the Ten greater weight as an interlocutor in the foreign policy field;
- closer cooperation in diplomatic and administrative matters between the missions of the Ten in third countries;
- the search for common positions at major international conferences attended by one or more of the Ten and covering questions dealt with in Political Cooperation;

- increasing recognition of the contribution which the European Parliament makes to the development of a coordinated foreign policy of the Ten.

First Report of the Foreign Ministers to the Heads of State and Government of the Member States of the European Community of 27 October 1970 (Luxembourg Report)

Under the chairmanship of the Federal Minister for Foreign Affairs, Walter Scheel, the Foreign Ministers of the six European Community countries, on 27 October 1970, in Luxembourg, finally approved, on behalf of their Governments, the report made pursuant to para. 15 of the Communiqué of The Hague on 20 July 1970.

The Foreign Ministers agreed to publish the report on 30 October 1970. The following is the text of the report:

Part One

1. The Ministers for Foreign Affairs of the Member States of the European Communities were instructed by the Heads of State or Government who met at The Hague on 1 and 2 December 1969 "to study the best way of achieving progress in the matter of political unification, within the context of enlargement" of the European Communities.

2. In carrying out this mandate, the Ministers were anxious to preserve the spirit of The Hague Communiqué. In it the Heads of State or Government noted in particular that with the entry into the final phase of the Common Market the building of Europe had reached "a turning point in its history"; they affirmed that "the European Communities remain the original nucleus from which European unity has been developed and intensified"; finally, they expressed their determination "to pave the way for a united Europe capable of assuming its responsibilities in the world of tomorrow and of making a contribution commensurate with its traditions and its mission."

3. The Heads of State or Government expressed their "common conviction that a Europe composed of States which, while preserving their national characteristics, are united in their essential interests, assured of internal cohesion, true to its friendly relations with outside countries, conscious of the role it has to play in promoting the relaxation of international tension and the rapprochement among all peoples, and first and foremost among those of the entire European continent, is indispensable if a mainspring of development, progress and culture, world equilibrium and peace is to be preserved."

4. A united Europe conscious of the responsibilities incumbent upon it by reason of its economic development, its industrial potential and its standard of living, intends to increase its efforts for the benefit of the developing countries with a view to establishing trustful relations among nations.

5. A united Europe must be founded upon the common heritage of respect for the liberty and the rights of men, and must assemble democratic States having freely elected parliaments. This united Europe remains the fundamental aim which should be achieved as soon as possible through the political will of its peoples and the decisions of their Governments.

6. Consequently, the Ministers held the view that for the sake of continuity and in order to meet the ultimate goal of political union in Europe, so strongly underlined by the Hague Conference, their proposals had to proceed from three considerations.

7. First, shape ought to be given, in the spirit of the preambles to the Treaties of Paris and Rome, to the will for political union which has not ceased to further the progress of the European Communities.

8. Second, the implementation of common policies already adopted or about to be adopted requires corresponding developments in the political sphere as such so that the time will come nearer when Europe will be able to speak with one voice. It is therefore important that the construction of Europe should proceed in successive stages and that the most appropriate method of, and instruments for, joint political action should gradually develop.

9. Third, Europe must prepare itself to exercise the responsibilities which to assume in the world is both its duty and a necessity on account of its greater cohesion and its increasingly important role.

10. The present development of the European Communities requires Member States to intensify their political co-operation and provide in an initial phase the mechanism for harmonizing their views regarding international affairs.

Thus, the Ministers felt that efforts ought first to concentrate specifically on the co-ordination of foreign policies in order to show the whole world that Europe has a political mission. For they are convinced that progress in this direction would favour the development of the Communities and make the Europeans more conscious of their common responsibility.

Part Two

The Ministers propose the following: Desirous of making progress in the field of political unification, the Governments decided to co-operate in the sphere of foreign policy.

I. *Objectives*

The objectives of this co-operation are as follows:

- to ensure through regular exchanges of information and consultations, a better mutual understanding on the great international problems; to strengthen their solidarity by promoting the harmonization of their views, the co-ordination of their positions, and, where it appears possible and desirable, to adopt a common position on international matters;
- common actions.

II. *Ministerial Meetings*

1. On the initiative of the Chairman, the Ministers for Foreign Affairs will meet at least every six months.

If they feel that the gravity of the circumstances or the importance of the subjects in question so justify, their meeting may be replaced by a conference of Heads of State or Government.

Should a grave crisis or a matter of particular urgency arise, extraordinary consultations will be arranged between the Governments of Member States. The Chairman will get in touch with his colleagues in order to determine the best way of ensuring such consultation.

2. The Minister for Foreign Affairs of the country having the chair in the Council of the European Communities will chair the meetings.

3. The ministerial meetings will be prepared by a committee composed of the Directors of political affairs.

III. *Political Committee*

1. A committee composed of the Directors of political affairs will meet at least four times a year to prepare the ministerial meetings and carry out any tasks delegated to them by the Ministers.

Further, the Chairman may, in exceptional cases, and after having consulted his colleagues, convene the Committee either on his own initiative or at the request of one of the members.

2. The chairmanship of the Committee will be subject to the same rules as those which apply to ministerial meetings.

3. The Committee may set up working groups to deal with special matters.

It may appoint a group of experts to collect material relating to a specific problem and to present the possible alternatives.

4. Any other form of consultation may be envisaged where necessary.

IV. Subjects for Consultations

Governments will consult on all important questions of foreign policy.

Member States may propose any question of their choice for political consultation.

V. Commission of the European Communities

Should the work of the Minister affect the activities of the European Communities, the Commission will be invited to make known its views.

VI. European Parliamentary Assembly

In order to give a democratic character to political unification, it will be necessary to associate public opinion and its representatives with it.

The Ministers and members of the Political Commission of the European Parliamentary Assembly will meet for a biannual colloquy to discuss questions that are the subject of consultation within the framework of co-operation on foreign affairs. This colloquy will be held in an informal way to give parliamentarians and Ministers an opportunity freely to express their opinions.

VII. General Provisions

1. The meetings will as a general rule be held in the country whose representative is in the chair.

2. The host country will make the necessary arrangements to provide the secretariat and the material organization of the meetings.

3. Each country will designate an official of its Ministry of Foreign Affairs who will liaise with his counterparts in the other countries.

Part Three

1. In order to ensure continuity in the task undertaken, the Ministers propose to pursue their study on the best way of achieving progress in the field of political unification, and to present a second report.

2. This study will also deal with the improvement of co-operation in foreign policy matters and with the search for other fields where progress might be achieved. This study must take into account work undertaken within the European Communites especially with a view to reinforcing their structures and thus, if need be, to enable them to live up to their increasing and developing tasks.

3. To this end, the Ministers instruct the Political Committee to arrange its activities in such a way that it will be able to fulfill this

task, and to present a summary report at each biannual ministerial meeting.

4. The Chairman of the Council will once a year address a communication to the European Parliamentary Assembly on progress in that work.

5. Notwithstanding any interim reports which they may consider worth submitting if their deliberations so permit, the Ministers for Foreign Affairs will present their second full report not later than two years after the commencement of consultations on foreign policy. That report must contain an assessment of the results obtained by those consultations.

Part Four

Proposals concerning association of the applicant countries with the work envisaged in part II and III of the Report.

1. The Ministers emphasize that there is a correlation between membership in the European Communities and participation in the activities designed to help achieve progress in the field of political unification.

2. Since the applicant countries must be consulted on the objectives and procedures described in the present Report, and since they must adhere to them once they have become members of the European Communities, it is necessary to keep those countries informed of progress in the work of the Six.

3. In view of those different objectives the following procedures for informing the applicant countries are suggested:

(a) Meetings of the Ministers:

At each of their biannual meetings the Ministers will fix the day of their next meeting.

They will at the same time propose a date for ministerial meeting of the Ten. That date shall be as close as possible to that of the meeting of the Six and shall normally be after it; in fixing that date such occasions shall be borne in mind when the ten Ministers or some of them meet anyhow.

After the ministerial meeting of the Six the Chairman shall inform the applicant countries of the questions which the Ministers propose to put on the agenda of the ministerial meeting of the Ten, and shall furnish them all other information likely to make the exchange of views of the Ten as fruitful as possible.

In view of the fact that the information and the exchange of views must be marked by a certain flexibility, it is understood that they will be intensified once the agreements on the applicant countries' accession to the European Communities have been signed.

(b) Meetings of the Political Committee:

This Committee will furnish the applicant countries the information likely to be of interest to them. The information shall be transmitted by the Chair to whom those countries shall address their response, if any. The Chair will report on it to the Political Committee.

Statement of the Conference of the Heads of State and Government of the Member States of the European Community (Paris, 21 October 1972)

The Heads of State or of Government of the Countries of the Enlarged Community, meeting for the First Time on 19 and 20 October in Paris, at the Invitation of the President of the French Republic, solemnly declare:

at the moment when enlargement, decided in accordance with the rules in the Treaties and with respect for what the six original Member States have already achieved, is to become a reality and to give a new dimension to the Community;

at a time when world events are profoundly changing the international situation;

now that there is a general desire for détente and cooperation in response to the interest and the wishes of all peoples;

now that serious monetary and trade problems require a search for lasting solutions that will favour growth with stability;

now that many developing countries see the gap widening between themselves and the industrial nations and claim with justification an increase in aid and a fairer use of wealth;

now that the tasks of the Community are growing, and fresh responsibilities are being laid upon it, the time has come for Europe to recognize clearly the unity of its interests, the extent of its capacities and the magnitude of its duties; Europe must be able to make its voice heard in world affairs. . . .

Second Report of the Foreign Ministers to the Heads of State and Government of the Member States of the European Community of 23 July 1973 (Copenhagen Report)

The Foreign Ministers of the nine Member States of the European Communities, in carrying out the instruction given them in para. 14 of the Declaration of the Paris Summit Conference of 21 October 1972, have submitted the second report on the European Political Co-operation. The Heads of State and Government have approved the report.

The following is the text of the report:

Part I

The Heads of State or of Government of the Member States of the European Communities approved on 27 October 1970 the Report of the Foreign Ministers drawn up in implementation of paragraph 15 of the Communiqué of the Hague Conference of 1 and 2 December 1969. The document reflected the belief that progress towards concerted action in the field of foreign policy was likely to promote the development of the Communities and to help the Europeans to realize more fully their common responsibilities. The objectives of the co-operation are:

- to ensure by means of regular consultations and exchanges of information, improved mutual understanding as regards the main problems of international relations;
- to strengthen solidarity between Governments by promoting the harmonization of their views and the alignment of their positions and, wherever it appears possible and desirable, joint action.

The Report also proposed that the Foreign Ministers should submit a second general report which would *inter alia*, contain an assessment of the results obtained from such consultation. At the time when the enlargement of the European Communities became a fact, paragraph 14 of the Summit Declaration in Paris on 21 October 1972 required the Foreign Ministers to produce by 30 June 1973 a second report on methods of improving political co-operation in accordance with the Luxembourg Report.

The Heads of State or of Government, meeting in Paris, expressed their satisfaction at the results obtained since the political co-operation machinery was formally set up on the basis of the texts of 27 October 1970. In several fields, the Member States have been able to consider and decide matters jointly so as to make common political action possible. This habit has also led to the "reflex" of co-ordination among the Member States which has profoundly affected the relations of the Member States between each other and with third countries. This collegiate sense in Europe is becoming a real force in international relations.

The Ministers note that the characteristically pragmatic mechanisms set up by the Luxembourg Report have shown their flexibility and effectiveness. What is involved in fact is a new procedure in international relations and an original European contribution to the technique of arriving at concerted action. The experience acquired so far has resulted in a strengthening of the belief in the usefulness of concerted action by means of direct contact beteen senior officials of Foreign Ministries and of a very thorough preparation of the matters under consideration as a basis for the decisions by Ministers.

Such concerted action has also had a positive influence in so far as it has brought a more conscious collaboration between representatives of Member States of the Communities in third countries. They have been encouraged to meet and compare the information available to them. This habit of working together has enabled the procedure for concerted action to become more widespread wherever common action or common consideration seemed desirable.

In the Luxembourg Report provision was made for the Commission to be invited to make known its views when the work of the Ministers affected the activities of the European Communities. The Foreign Ministers express satisfaction that these contacts have now become a reality and that a constructive and continuing dialogue is in course both at the level of experts and of the Political Committee, and at ministerial meetings.

The colloquy with the Political Commission of the European Parliament and the communication by the President of the Council to the European Parliament have put into effect the desire of the Foreign Ministers to make a contribution to the democratic character of the construction of political union.

The final Declaration of the Conference of Heads of State or of Government held on 19–21 October 1972 expressed, *inter alia*, the conviction that Europe must be able to make its voice heard in world affairs and to affirm its own views in international relations.

Europe now needs to establish its position in the world as a distinct entity, especially in international negotiations which are likely to have a decisive influence on the international equilibrium and on the future of the European Community.

In the light of this it is essential that, in the spirit of the conclusions of the Paris Summit Conference, co-operation among the Nine on foreign policy should be such as to enable Europe to make an original contribution to the international equilibrium. Europe has the will to do this, in accordance with its traditionally outward-looking mission and its interest in progress, peace and co-operation. It will do so, loyal to its traditional friends and to the alliances of its Member States, in the spirit of good neighbourliness which must exist between all the countries of Europe both to the east and the west, and responding to the expectations of all the developing countries.

The results obtained by the procedure of political consultation since its inception, referred to in the preceding paragraphs, are the subject of a descriptive Annex attached to this Report.

Part II

In implementation of the task entrusted to them by paragraph 14 of the Paris Summit Declaration, and having regard to the objective which the Heads of State or of Government set themselves, namely to transform before the end of the present decade, the whole complex of the relations between the Member States of the European Communities into a European Union, the Foreign Ministers propose that the Heads of State or of Government approve the following measures:

1. Ministerial Meetings

Henceforth, the Foreign Ministers will meet four times a year. They may also, whenever they consider it necessary to consult each other on specific subjects between meetings, meet for that purpose when they happen to come together on other occasions.

2. The Political Committee of the Member States of the European Communities

The Political Directors of the Member States of the Community will meet in the Political Committee of the Member States of the European Communities with a view to preparing ministerial meetings and carrying out tasks entrusted to them by the Ministers. In order to attain that objective, meetings of the Committee will be held as frequently as the intensification of the work requires.

3. The Group of "Correspondents"

A group consisting of European "Correspondents" in the Foreign Ministry (called the Group of Correspondents) will be set up. That Group will be entrusted with the task of following the implementation of political co-operation and of studying problems of organization and problems of a general nature. Furthermore, for certain matters, the Group will prepare the work of the Political Committee on the basis of instruction given by that Committee.

4. *Working Parties*

(a) In order to ensure more thorough consultation on individual questions, working parties will be set up to bring together senior officials of the Ministries of Foreign Affairs responsible for the subject under consideration. These working parties will cease to meet as soon as they have completed the task entrusted to them. Exceptionally, and especially in order to ensure continuity if the work can be completed in the near future, the chairman of a working party may be required to continue in office beyond the usual period.

(b) The chairman in office may approach the Political Committee about the need to bring together senior officials of the major ministerial departments who have not met during the preceding six month period with a view to keeping them in contact with each other.

5. *Medium- and Long-Term Studies*

In accordance with paragraph 14 of the Declaration of the Paris Summit Conference, which set as an objective on political co-operation the formulation, where possible, of common medium and long term positions, several methods of work can be envisaged. According to circumstances, this will be done either by groups of experts in addition to the current matters which they normally deal with, or by entrusting the preparations of such studies to a special analysis and research group consisting normally of officials.

The Political Committee will propose to the Foreign Ministers specific subjects for study.

6. *The Role of the Embassies of the Nine in*
the Capitals of the Member-Countries of the Community

The Embassies of the Nine participate closely in the implementation of political co-operation. In particular, they receive information on a Community basis issued by the Foreign Ministry of their country of residence. Furthermore, they are occasionally entrusted with consultations on specific subjects:

- at the seat of the Presidency at the request of the Political Committee, the Presidency or another Member State; or
- in another Capital at the request of the Foreign Ministry.

They will appoint one of their diplomatic staff who will specifically be entrusted with ensuring the necessary contacts with the Foreign Ministry of their country of residence, within the framework of political co-operation.

7. Roles of the Embassies in Third Countries and of the Offices of Permanent Representatives to Major International Organizations

With the introduction of the political co-operation machinery, it proved useful to associate Embassies and Permanent Representatives' offices with the work. In the light of the experience gained, better information on the work in progress in the field of political co-operation should be provided so as to enable them, where necessary, to put forward in an appropriate form those aspects which they consider of interest for this work, including considerations on joint action.

With this in mind, the Political Committee will notify the missions concerned when it considers it necessary to obtain a contribution on a specific item of its agenda. Where appropriate, it may require a common report to be prepared by them on specific questions.

In addition to the provisions contained in the texts in force governing reciprocal information on the occasion of important visits, the Ambassador concerned, accredited in the country where the visit takes place, should first provide information to his colleagues on the spot so as to enable any appropriate exchange of views. After the visit, such information as may interest them should be given to them in the most appropriate manner.

Finally, in application of the provisions governing the role of missions abroad, the permanent representatives of the Member States to the major international organizations will regularly consider matters together and, on the basis of instructions received, will seek common positions in regard to important questions dealt with by those organizations.

8. The Presidency

As regards the internal organization of the work of political co-operation, the Presidency:

- sees to it that the conclusions adopted at meetings of Ministers and of the Political Committee are implemented on a collegiate basis;
- proposes, on its own initiative or on that of another State, consultation at an appropriate level;

- may also, between meetings of the Political Committee, meet the Ambassadors of the Member States in order to inform them of the progress of the work of political co-operation. The meeting may take place at the request of an Ambassador of a Member State seeking consultation on a specific subject.

Experience has also shown that the Presidency's task presents a particularly heavy administrative burden. Administrative assistance may therefore be provided by other Member States for specific tasks.

9. Improvement of Contact Between the Nine

The Foreign Ministers have agreed to establish a communications system with a view to facilitating direct contact between their departments.

10. Relations with the European Parliament

Having regard to the widening scope of the European Communities and the intensification of political co-operation at all levels, four colloquies will be held each year at which the Ministers will meet with members of the Political Committee of the European Parliament. For the purpose of preparing the colloquies, the Political Committee will draw to the attention of Ministers proposals adopted by the European Parliament on foreign policy questions.

In addition the Minister exercising the function of President will continue, as in the past, to submit to the European Parliament, once a year, a communication on progress made in the field of political co-operation.

11. Priorities To Be Set in Respect of the Matters To Be Dealt with Within the Framework of Political Co-operation

Governments will consult each other on all important foreign policy questions and will work out priorities, observing the following criteria:

- the purpose of the consultation is to seek common policies on practical problems;
- the subject dealt with must concern European interests whether in Europe itself or elsewhere where the adoption of a common position is necessary or desirable.

On these questions each State undertakes as a general rule not to take up final positions without prior consultation with its partners within the framework of the political co-operation machinery.

The Political Committee will submit to the meetings of Foreign Ministers subjects among which the Ministers may select those to be given priority in the course of political co-operation. This is without prejudice to the examination of additional subjects either at the suggestion of a Member State or as a result of recent developments.

12. Relationship Between the Work of the Political Cooperation Machinery and That Carried Out Within the Framework of the European Communities

(a) The Political Co-operation machinery, which deals on the intergovernmental level with problems of international politics, is distinct from and additional to the activities of the institutions of the Community which are based on the juridical commitments undertaken by the Member States in the Treaty of Rome. Both sets of machinery have the aim of contributing to the development of European unification. The relationship between them is discussed below.

(b) The Political Co-operation machinery, which is responsible for dealing with questions of current interest and where possible for formulating common medium and long term positions, must do this keeping in mind, *inter alia*, the implications for and the effects of, in the field of international politics, Community policies under construction.

For matters which have an incidence on Community activities close contact will be maintained with the institutions of the Community.

(c) The last section of the previous paragraph is implemented in the following way;

- the Commission is invited to make known its views in accordance with current practice;
- the Council, through the President of the Committee of Permanent Representatives, is informed by the Presidency of the agreed conclusions which result from the work of the Political Co-operation machinery, to the extent that these conclusions have an interest for the work of the Community;
- the Ministers will similarly be able, if it is so desired, to instruct the Political Co-operation machinery to prepare studies on certain political aspects of problems under examination in the framework of the Community. These reports will be transmitted to the Council through the President of the Committee of Permanent Representatives.

In drawing up this Report, the Ministers have demonstrated their belief that even more important than the contents of their proposals is the spirit in which these are put into effect. That spirit is the one that emerges from the decisions taken at the Paris Summit meeting.

The Ministers consider that co-operation on foreign policy must be placed in the perspective of European Union.

From now on, it is of the greatest importance to seek common positions on major international problems.

Annex

Results obtained from European Political Co-operation on Foreign Policy.

1. Ministerial Meetings
(Luxembourg Report—Second Part, II)

As from the second half of 1970, the Ministers for Foreign Affairs of Member States of the European Communities have met regularly twice a year.

In pursuance of the decision taken by the Conference of Heads of State or of Government in Paris on 19–20 October 1972, the number of these meetings has, from 1973, been increased from two to four.

2. Political Committee
(Luxembourg Report–Second Part, III)

(a) The Luxembourg Report provided for at least four meetings a year. From the outset, the Political Committee met more often than had been foreseen; in fact, during the last twelve months, it has held nine meetings.

(b) The Political Committee has noted that the aims defined in the Luxembourg Report could only be achieved by adequate preparation. To this effect and without thereby discarding other possible formulas, it has established within the framework of its activities, working parties entrusted with particular tasks:

- a Sub-Committee was set up to study problems relating to the Conference on Security and Co-operation in Europe (CSCE), and an *ad hoc* Group, in which the Commission of the European Communities takes part, was set up to examine the economic aspects. In view of the need for such studies, it was decided that the Sub-Committee and the *ad hoc* Group should meet on a permanent basis in Helsinki in order to work, on the spot, for agreed positions in response to developments in the negotiations;
- three working parties were set up with a view to following and studying problems relating, respectively, to the situation in the Middle East, the Mediterranean area and Asia; senior officials in

the Foreign Ministries with responsibility for those questions usually participate in this work;

- there were also meetings of experts dealing with various questions as, for example, co-operation in the event of natural disasters;
- consultations also took place between the Presidency and the Embassies of Member States on the situation in the Indian sub-continent and in the Middle East.

(c) Furthermore, it was decided to place within the framework of political co-operation the consultations which used to take place within the WEU before sessions of the General Assembly of the United Nations, of the Economic and Social Council and of the FAO. For this purpose, alongside the co-ordination meetings of the Permanent Representatives, senior officials responsible for the different sectors within each of the national Administrations get together to discuss certain items placed on the Agendas of these sessions; they report to the Political Committee.

3. Group of "Correspondents"
(Luxembourg Report—Second Part, VII-3)

In order to facilitate the internal organization of political co-operation, the Luxembourg Report provided that each State should appoint from within its Ministry of Foreign Affairs an official who should act as the "correspondant" of his opposite numbers in other States. These officials were established as a "Group of Correspondents"; this Group, in addition to the task of drafting summaries of the conclusions reached at ministerial meetings and meetings of the Political Committee, was entrusted with the duty of closely following the implementation of political co-operation and of studying the problems of organization and those of a general nature, as well as particular problems the Political Committee gave it to examine, in particular for the purpose of preparing their meetings.

4. Activities of Embassies of the Nine in the
Capitals of Member States of the Communities

The role of Ambassadors of the nine in the capitals of Member States has proved important for the implementation of political co-operation in particular with respect to the exchange of information. In order to facilitate contacts with the Ministries of Foreign Affairs in the countries of their residence with respect to matters of political co-operation, each of these Embassies has appointed a diplomat on its staff whose special duty is to ensure contact with the Ministry of Foreign Affairs in its country of residence on matters of political co-operation.

Since the Ambassadors receive information concerning the Community from the Ministry of Foreign Affairs of their country of residence and, in particular, since they are expected by the Political Committee to engage in discussions from time to time, in the capital of the Presidency, it is important that they should be fully informed of the progress of political co-operation with the implementation of which their missions are associated.

5. Association of Ambassadors in Third Countries and of Permanent Representatives to International Organizations with the Political Co-operation

It has been judged necessary and in line with the Luxembourg Report to associate Heads of the diplomatic missions of the Nine with political co-operation. For that purpose, it has been arranged that the Political Committee can ask Ambassadors accredited to a particular country to provide it with reports and thus to encourage co-operation among the diplomatic representatives of Member States.

It had also been arranged that regular discussion can take place between Ambassadors accredited to countries other than those of the Community, on problems of common interest concerning the country to which they are accredited, in accordance with such procedures as the Ambassadors themselves would find appropriate.

These provisions were put into operation and developed during the first two years of political co-operation.

Heads of diplomatic missions in many posts, or their representatives, while taking account of local conditions, take part increasingly in political co-operation, especially through exchanges of view and in certain cases by means of joint reports.

6. Commission of the European Communities (Luxembourg Report—Second Part, V)

The Luxembourg Report provides that:

> should the work of the Ministers affect the activities of the European Communities, the Commission will be invited to make known its views.

In accordance with this the Commission of the Communities has been invited to participate in ministerial discussions and in sessions of the Political Committee and of groups of experts when the agenda of the meetings provides for the examination of questions affecting the activities of the Communities; for example, the examination of problems relating to the economic aspects of the CSCE and to the future role of the Council of Europe.

7. European Parliament
(Luxembourg Report—Second Part, VI, and Third Part, 4)

In accordance with the Luxembourg Report which provided for two methods of associating public opinion and in representatives with the development of political co-operation, Ministers for Foreign Affairs and members of the Political Commission of the European Parliament held a colloquy every six months and the President in office of the Council reported every year to the Parliament on the progress of work concerning the best means of advancing towards political union.

At the last two colloquies, a new procedure, consisting essentially of the notification in advance to the Political Commission of the European Parliament of the main subjects for discussion, was adopted in order to make the exchange of views more fruitful.

8. Participation of New Members

Political co-operation was started when the European Communities consisted of only six members—the applicant States being associated with their activities in accordance with the procedure specified in the fourth part of the Luxembourg Report. The procedure provided that the Ministers of the Six would meet their colleagues from acceding States at a time as near as possible to their meetings in order to ensure necessary consultation for keeping those States informed of the progress of the work of the Six.

Similarly, it was arranged for the President in office of the Political Committee to communicate to applicant States information likely to interest them and for him to obtain any reactions they had. This rule was adopted to take account of the essential connection between membership of the European Communities and participation in activities enabling further progress to be made towards political union.

After signature of the Act of Accession on 22 January, 1972, these States have fully participated in meetings at every level.

Report on European Political Cooperation
(London, 13 October 1981)

The Foreign Ministers of the ten Member States of the European Community have examined the development of European political cooperation. It is their constant concern that this should be improved, and to this end they have considered how it might be further strengthened.

Political cooperation, which is based on membership of the European Community, has developed to become a central element in the foreign policies of all Member States. The Community and its Member States are increasingly seen by third countries as a coherent force in international relations. The Foreign Ministers of the Ten note that in the years since the foundations of European political cooperation were laid in the Luxembourg Report (approved by Heads of State and Government on 27 October 1970) and the Copenhagen Report (approved by Foreign Ministers on 23 July 1973 and subsequently agreed by Heads of State and Government) significant progress has been achieved towards the objectives set out in those reports.

The development of European political cooperation over these years has shown that it answers a real need felt by the Member States of the European Community for a closer unity in this field. It is a mark of its proven value that European political cooperation has steadily intensified and its scope continually broadened. This development has contributed to the ultimate objective of European union.

The Foreign Ministers agree that further European integration, and the maintenance and development of Community policies in accordance with the Treaties, will be beneficial to a more effective coordination in the field of foreign policy and will expand the range of instruments at the disposal of the Ten.

The Foreign Ministers believe that in a period of increased world tension and uncertainty the need for a coherent and united approach to international affairs by the members of the European Community is greater than ever. They note that, in spite of what has been achieved, the Ten are still far from playing a role in the world appropriate to their combined influence. It is their conviction that the Ten should seek increasingly to shape events and not merely to react to them.

As regards the scope of European political cooperation, and having regard to the different situations of the Member States, the Foreign Ministers agree to maintain the flexible and pragmatic approach which has made it possible to discuss in political cooperation certain important foreign policy questions bearing on the political aspects of security.

The ten Foreign Ministers also consider it timely to renew their commitment to implement fully the undertakings in the Luxembourg and Copenhagen Reports. In particular they underline the importance of consultation among the Ten, which lies at the heart of European political cooperation. They emphasize their commitment to consult partners before adopting final positions or launching national initiatives on all important questions of foreign policy which are of concern to the Ten as a whole. They undertake that in these consultations each Member State will take full account of the position of other partners and will give due weight to the desirability of achieving a common position. They note that such consultations will be particularly relevant for important international conferences where one or more of the Ten are to participate, and where the agenda will include matters under discussion in European political cooperation or on which the Ten have a common position.

The Foreign Ministers note that it is increasingly possible for the Ten to speak with one voice in international affairs. Where substantial common positions have been achieved, they undertake to give due prominence to these by means of appropriate references in national statements on foreign policy questions. At the same time they emphasize that not merely a common attitude but joint action, which has always been an objective of European political cooperation, should be increasingly within the capacity of the Ten.

The Foreign Ministers have also examined the machinery and procedures of political cooperation and have agreed on certain practical improvements which are set out in the following part of this document.

Ministerial Meetings

Formal Meetings

1. The agenda for meetings at ministerial level will include only items of major importance. The agenda will, where possible, also be annotated in such a way that the discussion will concentrate on matters for decision.

The analyses and draft texts submitted to ministers should contain either precise recommendations or clearly defined options so that the ministers can make decisions for future action.

When declarations are issued by ministerial meetings and the European Council, they should as a rule be accompanied by a list of posts in third countries where the local representative of the Ten will draw the declaration to the attention of the host government. In the absence of such a list the Presidency has discretion to take action on its own initiative.

Gymnich-type Meetings

In order to protect the informal character of these meetings, the following guidelines should be observed:

• Consultations are confidential.

- There will be no formal agenda, official interpretation or officials present (except for a presidency notetaker).
- The Presidency will summarize for the attention of partners any guidelines of an operational nature that emerge from the meeting.
- The press will only be briefed on subjects authorized by the Ten. The Presidency will be responsible in the first instance for such briefing, the lines of which will be agreed in advance with partners.

The Political Committee

2. The Political Committee is one of the central organs of European political cooperation. It is responsible for directing the work of the working groups and for the preparation of discussions at ministerial level.

The Political Committee will ensure the effective operation of working groups by giving them a clear mandate to report on matters of current interest. The Presidency will make the proposals necessary to achieve this. The working groups will however, remain free to suggest topics for reports to the Political Committee.

The Correspondents' Group

3. In order to permit the Political Committee to focus on the more important items on its agenda the European correspondents will identify those working group reports which are not likely to require substantive discussion in the Political Committee.

Working Groups

4. Working groups' reports will include a summary drawing the attention of the Political Committee to points which will require decisions for future action, or on which the Political Committee should concentrate.

In general, partners' comments via the COREU system on the oral reports of working groups should concentrate on points of substance and not of drafting.

If the Presidency considers a partner to be particularly well qualified on an agenda point at a working group meeting, it may request that partner to introduce the discussion on that topic.

Studies

5. Even when partners do not hold the Presidency, they should be encouraged to offer proposals and ideas for consideration by the working groups.

At present most of the efforts of political cooperation are devoted to reacting to world events as they occur. In future the Political Committee may wish to take a longer-term approach to certain problems, and to institute studies to that end. Such studies are already mentioned in the Copenhagen Report (Part II, paragraph 15) and should wherever possible be undertaken by existing working groups.

The Ten may also prepare studies on areas where their positions diverge (e.g. subjects on which they do not vote unanimously at the United Nations).

It is particularly important that the confidentiality of these studies should be maintained.

Confidentiality

6. The success of the process of political cooperation depends to a large degree on its confidentiality; certain particularly delicate matters need to be handled in a way which guarantees that the required level of confidentiality is maintained. In such cases papers will be transmitted to the foreign ministries via embassies, and distributed within foreign ministries by the European correspondent.

Procedures for EPC/Third Country Contacts

7. As European political cooperation intensifies and broadens, the Ten as such will appear as significant interlocuters. Third countries will increasingly express the desire to enter into more or less regular contact with them. It is important that the Ten should be able to respond effectively to these demands, in particular *vis-à-vis* countries of special interest to them, and that they should speak with one voice in dealings with them.

The Presidency may meet individual representatives of third countries in order to discuss certain matters of particular interest to the country in question.

The Presidency may respond to a request for contacts by a group of ambassadors of Member States of organizations with which the Ten maintains special links.

The Heads of Mission of the Ten in a country which expresses the desire for close contacts with EPC may meet representatives of that country in order to hear its views and to explain the position of the Ten.

If necessary, and if the Ten so agree, the Presidency, accompanied by representatives of the preceding and succeeding presidencies, may meet with representatives of third countries.

If necessary, and if the Ten so agree, the Presidency may meet the representative of a third country in the margins of a ministerial-level meeting of the Ten.

Procedure for Political Cooperation in Third Countries

8. In view of the increasing activities of the Ten in third countries, it is important that the Heads of Mission of the Ten maintain the practice of meeting regularly in order to exchange information and coordinate views. In considering their response to significant developments in the country to which they are accredited, their first instinct should be to coordinate with their colleagues of the Ten.

The participation of the head of Mission at political cooperation meetings should remain the rule. When this is impossible he may be represented by a member of his Mission.

The Political Committee welcomes joint reports from Heads of Missions of the Ten. These may be prepared in response to a request from the Political Committee or, exceptionally, on the Heads of Missions' own initiative, when the situation requires it. Recommendations for joint action are particularly valuable.

Where reports are made on the Heads of Missions' own initiative, it is for them to decide whether to draft a joint report or to report separately on the basis of their joint discussions. An equally acceptable alternative is for the Presidency to draft an oral report on its own authority reflecting the views expressed.

Contacts in the Capitals of the Ten

9. In certain capitals of the Ten the practice has developed of regular meetings between the nine Heads of Mission and the political director of the host government. This has proved useful and is to be encouraged.

The Presidency

10. As political cooperation has developed, the areas of agreement among the Ten have enlarged and the range of subjects handled has become more extensive. The workload of the Presidency in its role as spokesman in the European Parliament, and in contacts with third countries, has also increased. These trends may be expected to continue, particularly in the light of the enlargement of the Community.

As a result it has become desirable to strengthen the organization and assure the continuity of political cooperation and to provide operation support for the Presidency without, however, reducing the direct contact, pragmatism and economy which are among the chief virtues of the present arrangements.

Henceforth the Presidency will be assisted by a small team of officials seconded from preceding and succeeding presidencies. These officials will remain in the employment of their national foreign ministries, and will be on the staff of their embassy in the presidency capital. They will be at the disposition of the Presidency and will work under its direction.

The burden of work during the Presidency falls particularly heavily on the foreign minister who is President-in-Office. The Ten note that should he wish to do so the President may delegate certain tasks to his successor; he may also request his predecessor to finish tasks which are close to completion when the Presidency is handed over.

Relations with the European Parliament

11. In accordance with the Luxembourg and Copenhagen reports, which underline the importance of associating the European Parliament with political cooperation, there are frequent contacts between the European Parliament and the Presidency. These take the form of four annual colloquies with the Political Affairs Committee, answers to questions on political cooperation, the annual report on political cooperation, and the presidency speeches at the beginning and end of its term of office which now usually include political cooperation subjects.

The contacts between the Council of Ministers and the European Parliament have been extended to include informal meetings between ministers and the leaders of the different political groups represented in Parliament; these informal meetings provide a further opportunity for informal exchanges on political cooperation.

Taking account of the need to further strengthen ties with the directly-elected Parliament, the Ten envisage the possibililty of more frequent reference to resolutions adopted by Parliament in the deliberations, communiqués and declarations of the Ten, and in ministers' opening statements at colloquies with the Political Affairs Committee of Parliament.

The Ten note that after a meeting of the European Council the President of the European Council will make a statement to Parliament. This statement will include political cooperation subjects discussed at the meeting.

Relations Between the Activities of Political Cooperation and Those of the European Community

12. The Ten will provide, as appropriate, for political cooperation meetings on the occasion of Foreign Affairs Councils. The Presidency will ensure that the discussion of the community and political cooperation aspects of certain questions are coordinated if the subject-matter requires this.

Within the framework of the established rules and procedures the Ten attach importance to the Commission of the European Communities being fully associated with political cooperation, at all levels.

Crisis Procedures

13. The Political Committee, or, if necessary, a ministerial meeting will convene within forty-eight hours at the request of three Member States.

The same procedures will apply in third countries at the level of Heads of Mission.

In order to improve the capacity of the Ten to react in an emergency, working groups are encouraged to analyse areas of potential crisis and to prepare a range of possible reactions by the Ten.

Notes

1. This theme is discussed more fully in Weiler 1983. See also Cappelletti, Seccombe, and Weiler (forthcoming), which we have used and on which we have built.

2. Wheare 1963, at 169.

3. See Oliver 1974.

4. Of course there was an interest in questions of foreign trade even by constituent units.

5. The Soviet Union claimed some sort of federal foreign posture in conjunction with Byelorussia and the Ukraine. See Weiler 1983, p. 35 ff.

6. See note 4.

7. See Case 22/70 [1971] *European Court Reports* 263.

8. See Pescatore 1979.

9. See Bernier 1973.

10. The first agreement with Israel was concluded in 1964.

11. This was evident in the debate over the participation of the EEC in the Commodity Agreements: Opinion 1/78 [1979] ECR 2871.

12. Article 113 EEC, Rome Treaty.

13. Article 238 EEC, Rome Treaty.

14. Most First and Third World countries have legations to the EC.

15. See note 7.

16. See note 11.

17. For an up-to-date treatment on which we relied and a full bibliography, see Stein 1983.

18. See Greilsammer 1976.

19. See note 18.

20. See Weiler 1981.

21. Recalled in Stein 1983.

22. See Weiler 1982.

23. *London Report on European Political Cooperation.* 1981. Supplement 3 to Bulletin EC 6.

24. Von den Gablentz 1979.

25. See Stein 1983.

26. See text to note 23.

27. Although outside the treaty framework, the European Council is very much part of the EC machinery, a fact fully recognized in the Solemn Declaration, note 23.

28. See London Report 1981.

29. See Bonvicini 1977.

30. For a full discussion see Kauper 1982.
31. Ibid.
32. See Daintith 1982.
33. This view is explained and rejected in Allen, Rummel, Wessels 1982.
34. Elazar 1979b.
35. Pescatore 1982.
36. Elazar 1979a.
37. See Greilsammer 1981.
38. *Le Monde*, 1, 18–19 June 1967.
39. See, for example, Couve de Murville, pp. 463–475; and documents in "La politique étrangère de la France, textes et documents," *Notes et Etudes Documentaires* (La Documentation Française) nos. 3428–3430, 24 October 1967.
40. See Geiss 1967; and documents in Vogel 1967.
41. See Silvestri 1972; Biber 1967.
42. See Michel Vincineau 1973.
43. *Le Monde*, 30 June 1967.
44. *Le Monde*, 11 January 1971.
45. *Jewish Chronicle*, 27 November 1970.
46. *France-Soir*, 11 May 1971; *Jerusalem Post*, 12 May 1971.
47. *Welt am Sonntag*, quoted in *Jerusalem Post*, 12 July 1971; and *Die Welt* quoted in *Jerusalem Post* and *Le Monde*, 16 July 1971. On the Schumann Document see Kolodziej 1974, pp. 510–20.
48. See *Combat*, 13 May 1971; *Le Monde*, 13 May 1971 and 2 August 1971. Great Britain, which was not a member state of the Community at the time, also supported the Schumann Document. On the political "conditions" of Britain joining the EEC (in 1972), see Kitzinger 1973, pp. 59–76.
49. See *Le Monde*, 22 May 1971; *Combat*, 28 May 1971 and 13 June 1971.
50. Goodwin 1973, pp. 7–27. At the same time, several Europeans advocated a strong pro-Arab policy. See for example Girmont 1979.
51. *Le Monde*, 8–9 June 1973. *Le Nouvel Observateur*, 18 June 1973.
52. See De la Serre 1974; Lieber 1976; van Wel 1976.
53. See *Le Monde* 10 October 1973; 2 November 1973.
54. Geneviève Bibes, 1974.
55. *Le Monde*, 26 November 1973.
56. For a good description of French foreign policy towards the Middle East crisis in 1973, see Jobert 1974, p. 259 ff. And for a general analysis of the attitude of the Community see the special issue of *Revue Française de Science Politique*, 14 no. 4, April 1974; and 1975.
57. *Le Monde*, 8 November 1973; *Jerusalem Post*, 11 November 1973.
58. *Le Monde*, 11 November 1973.
59. See "La Cohésion des Neuf à l'ONU", *Trente Jours d'Europe*, no. 238, May 1978, pp. 23–32.
60. See the colloquium *Cooperazione e Sicurezza Nel Mediterraneo*, Rome, Ipalmo 1976; Hubert 1977; Meyer 1978; Allen 1978; Bourrinet 1979; Corbineau 1980.
61. See Greilsammer 1981; Giersch 1980; Cohen 1979.

62. See, for example, Halpern 1978.

63. See *European Stance on the Palestinian Issue*, 1977. For two good studies of the state of the European political cooperation process at the time of the London Declaration, see Allen 1978; Wallace 1977.

64. See *The EEC and the Middle East Peace Process*, London, Institute of Jewish Affairs, 1979, I.J.A. Research Report ME 79/5.

65. *Keesing's Contemporary Archives*, 1978, p. 29162.

66. *The EEC and the Middle East Peace Process*, 1979, p. 4.

67. *Bulletin of the European Community*, 1978, *Times*, 20 September 1978.

68. *Bulletin of the European Community*, March 1979; *Jewish Telegraphic Agency*, 28 March 1979; *Jewish Chronicle*, 30 March 1979.

69. *Bulletin of the European Community*, June 1979; *International Herald Tribune*, 19 June 1979.

70. For a discussion of the concept of self-determination, see for example Ronen 1979.

71. *Europe*, 6 June 1980.

72. *Europe*, 2–3 June 1980.

73. *Europe*, 11 June 1980.

74. *Europe*, 4 June 1980.

75. *Europe*, 5 June 1980; no. 2922, 6 June 1980.

76. *Le Soir*, 12 June 1980.

77. See, for example, *Europe*, 14 June 1980; *Middle East International*, 30 October 1981; *Daily Express*, 14 June 1980. For a discussion, see Allen and Smith 1983.

78. *Daily Telegraph*, 16 June 1980.

79. *International Herald Tribune*, 16 June 1980.

80. *Daily Express*, 14 June 1980.

81. *International Herald Tribune*, 16 June 1980.

82. *La Dernière Heure*, 17 June 1980.

83. *Scotsman*, 17 June 1980.

84. *Daily Telegraph*, 16 June 1980; *International Herald Tribune*, 16 June 1980.

85. *Middle East International*, 18 July 1980.

86. *Le Nouveau Journal*, 24 July 1980.

87. *Europe*, 31 July 1980.

88. *Europe*, 29 August 1980.

89. *La Libre Belgique*, 17 June 1980.

90. *Europe*, 14, 15 July 1980; *Financial Times*, 21 July 1980.

91. *International Herald Tribune*, 2, 3 August 1980.

92. *Europe*, no. 2956, 25 July 1980; 30 July 1980.

93. *La Cité*, 31 July 1980; *Le Soir*, 31 July 1980.

94. *Times*, 5 August 1980.

95. *Europe*, 2 August 1980.

96. *Le Monde*, 7 August 1980; *Europe*, no. 2963, 25, 26 August 1980.

97. *La Libre Belgique*, 29 August 1980; *Guardian*, 3 September 1980.

98. *Europe*, 1, 2 September 1980; no. 2970, 4 September 1980.

99. *Guardian*, 5 September 1980.

100. *Europe*, no. 2989, 1 October 1980; *Le Soir*, 1 October 1980; *International Herald Tribune*, 1 October 1980; *Le Figaro*, 2 October 1980.

101. *Guardian*, 13 October 1980.

102. *Europe*, 17 September 1980.

103. *Europe*, 27, 28 October 1980.

104. Quoted in *Le Monde*, 15 November 1980; comment in *Le Soir*, 15 November 1980. In general, see Garfinkle 1981.

105. *Le Monde*, 16, 17 November 1980.

106. *Le Monde*, 18 November 1980; *Europe*, no. 3022, 19 November 1980.

107. *Le Soir*, 26 November 1980.

108. *Times*, 2 December 1980.

109. *Europe*, 3 December 1980; and R. Calis in *The Middle East International*, January 1981.

110. *Europe*, 26 November 1980.

111. *Le Soir*, 28, 29 December 1980.

112. *International Herald Tribune*, 2 March 1981.

113. See *Le Soir*, 2 March 1981; *Times*, 5 March 1981; *Guardian*, 5 March 1981.

114. *Jerusalem Post*, 9, 12 January 1981.

115. *Europe*, 7 January 1981; *Times*, 7 January 1981; *Guardian*, 8 January 1981.

116. *Europe*, 18 February 1981.

117. *Europe*, 28 February 1981.

118. For a good analysis of the foreign policy program of the French Socialist party, when it was in the opposition, see Huntzinger 1978; Serfaty 1979.

119. *Europe*, 22 January 1981; no. 3064, 26, 27 January 1981.

120. *Europe*, 4 March 1981.

121. *Europe*, 8 November 1980; *Akhbar-Ouroubyia-Arabia* (Brussels), November 1980; *Europe*, 13 November 1980; *Europe*, 14 November 1980; *Financial Times*, 14 November 1980.

122. *Europe*, 11 February 1981.

123. *Europe*, 14 February 1982; 16, 17 February 1981.

124. *Le Matin*, 17 January 1981.

125. *Europe*, 2, 3 February 1981.

126. *Europe*, 14 February 1981.

127. *Europe*, 21, 22 April 1981. The Soviet Union insisted again on a full Israeli withdrawal from all occupied territories including Jerusalem, the establishment of a Palestinian state, the participation of the PLO in any peace negotiation, and the need for an international conference (with all the parties involved) to solve the Middle East conflict.

128. *Guardian*, 13 January 1981; *La Libre Belgique*, 13 January 1981.

129. *Europe*, no. 3090, 4 March 1981.

130. *Europe*, no. 3123, 21, 22 April 1981.

131. *Europe*, no. 3137, 13 May 1981.

132. *Europe*, 1 July 1981.

133. *Middle East International*, 3 July 1981.

134. *Middle East International*, no. 154, 17 July 1981.

135. *Europe*, 31 August 1981.

136. *Europe*, 9 December 1981; *Financial Times*, 9 December 1981.

137. *Le Républicain Lorrain*, 10 December 1981; *Le Soir*, 10 December 1981; *Le Figaro*, 10 December 1981; *Middle East International*, 11 December 1981.

138. *Europe*, 12 December 1981.

139. *Le Monde*, 11 December 1981.

140. *Le Monde*, 5 January 1982.

141. *Le Monde*, 23 February 1982.

142. *Europe*, 14 October 1981.

143. *Middle East International*, 30 October 1981.

144. *Europe*, 9, 10 November 1981.

145. *Europe*, 27 November 1981; *Middle East International*, 27 November 1981; *Le Monde*, 27 November 1981; *Guardian*, 28 November 1981.

146. *Europe*, 22 October 1981.

147. *Europe*, 23 October 1981; no. 3237, 26, 27 October 1981; 28 October 1981; 31 October 1981.

148. *Europe*, 25 November 1981.

149. *Europe*, 5 December 1981.

150. *Europe*, 15 January 1982.

151. See *Le Nouveau Journal*, 20 October 1981; *Financial Times*, 22–23 October 1981. On the representation of PASOK, the Greek Socialist party, at the European Parliament in Strasbourg, see *D'Letzeburger Land*, 23 October 1981.

152. *Times*, 23 November 1981.

153. See *Tribune Juive*, 30 October–5 November 1981; *Jerusalem Post* 15, 17 December 1981.

154. See *Europe*, 2, 3 November 1981; *Times*, 24 November 1981.

155. *Le Matin*, 7 June 1982.

156. *Le Monde*, 8 June 1982.

157. *Jerusalem Post*, 8 June 1982.

158. *Jerusalem Post*, 29 June 1982.

159. *Le Matin*, 8 June 1982; *Le Monde*, 8 June 1982.

160. *L'Humanité*, 9 June 1982.

161. *Le Soir*, 8 June 1982.

162. For a presentation of the thesis, according to which the Israeli action was a violation of international law, see the controversial. *Israel in Lebanon*, London, Ithaca Press, 1983.

163. *Agence Belga*, 9 June 1982; *Times*, 10 June 1982; *La Cité*, 11 June 1982; *Le Soir*, 12 June 1982.

164. *L'Humanité*, 16 June 1982, *Le Monde*, 16–17 June 1982.

165. *Le Monde*, 18 June 1982.

166. *Le Monde*, 19, 21 June 1982.

167. *Le Matin*, 26 June 1982; *Libération*, 26 June 1982; *Le Monde*, 26 June 1982.

168. See, for example, *International Herald Tribune*, 29 June 1982; *Irish Press*, 29 June 1982; *Le Quotidien de Paris*, 29 June 1982; *Daily Express*, 29 June 1982. For an Israeli perspective, see *Jerusalem Post*, 29, 30 June 1982.

169. See, for example, *Guardian*, 2 July 1982; *La Dernière Heure*, 2 July 1982.

170. *Le Matin*, 7 July 1982.

171. *Le Matin*, 8 July 1982; and on French reactions to the "Arafat Document", see *Libérations*, 29 July 1982; *Le Monde*, 28 July 1982.

172. *Le Quotidien de Paris*, 15 July 1982, *Libération*, 16 July 1982.

173. *Le Matin*, 12, 13 July 1982.

174. *Le Matin*, 16 August 1982.

175. *La Cité*, 17 July 1982; *Le Peuple*, 20 July 1982; *Financial Times*, 20 July 1982.

176. *Irish Times*, 20 July 1982; *Guardian*, 20 July 1982.

177. *Documents* of the 26th Meeting of the Extraordinary Session of the United Nations General Assembly, 1982 A/ES-7/PV26, pp. 13–17.

178. UN General Assembly, A/ES-7/PV 31, pp. 49–51.

179. UN General Assembly, A/ES-7/PV 28, pp. 7–10.

180. *Le Monde*, 3 September 1982.

181. *D'Letzeburger Land*, 24 September 1982.

182. See *Le Monde*, 3 September 1982.

183. *Financial Times*, 3 September 1982.

184. *Guardian*, 16 September 1982.

185. *Le Monde*, 4 September 1982.

186. *Le Monde*, 10 September 1982.

187. *La Dernière Heure*, 19 September 1982.

188. *Financial Times*, 29 September 1982.

189. *La Libre Belgique*, 30 September 1982.

190. *Le Soir*, 30 September 1982; *Times*, 30 September 1982.

191. *Le Matin*, 14 October 1982.

192. *Times*, 29 November 1982.

193. *Financial Times*, 6 December 1982; *Le Monde*, 7 December 1982.

194. *La Cité*, 2 December 1982.

195. *Le Soir*, 9 February 1983.

196. *Le Monde*, 17, 20, 21, 23, 24 February 1983; *Le Matin*, 22 February 1983.

197. *Républicain Lorrain*, 8 October 1982.

198. *Le Soir*, 22 March 1983; *La Libre Belgique*, 23 March 1983; *International Herald Tribune*, 23 March 1983.

199. *Times*, 23 March 1983.

200. *La Cité*, 23 March 1983.

201. *La Libre Belgique*, 23 March 1983.

202. Quoted by *Le Soir*, 24 March 1983.

203. *Le Monde*, 17 May 1983.

Bibliography

Allen, David. 1978. The Euro-Arab Dialogue. *Journal of Common Market Studies* 16, no. 4: 323–42.

Allen, David and Wolfgang Rummel, eds. 1982. *European Political Cooperation*. London: Butterworths.

Allen, David and Michael Smith. 1983. Europe, the United States and the Middle East: A Case Study in Comparative Policy Making. *Journal of Common Market Studies* 22, no. 2 (December): 125–46.

Bernier, Ivan. 1973. *International Legal Aspects of Federalism*. London: Croom Helm.

Bibes, Geneviève. 1967. L'Italie est partagée entre ses intérêts pétroliers et son attachement à l'Alliance atlantique. *Le Monde Diplomatique* (August): 8 ff.

Bibes, Geneviève. 1974. *L'Italie a-t-elle une politique étrangère?* Paris: Centre d'Etudes des Relations Internationales.

Bonvicini, Giovanni. 1977. The Problem of Coordination between Political Cooperation and Community Activities. *Lo Spettatore Internazionale* 12: 55.

Bourrinet, Jacques, ed. 1979. *Le dialogue Euro-Arabe*. Paris: Economica.

Bulletin of the European Community. 1978. European Community. Brussels.

Cappelletti, Mauro, Novice Seccombe, and Joseph Weiler. 1985. Introduction. In *Integration Through Law*. Berlin/New York: Walter de Groyter.

Cohen, Yaacov. 1979. *Israel's Intergration in the Economic Structure of the European Community*. Jerusalem: Ministry of Industry.

Corbineau, Bernard. 1980. Le dialogue euro-arabe. *Revue Française de Science Politique* 30, no. 3 (June): 560–98.

Couve de Murville, Maurice. 1971. *Une politique étrangere 1958–1969*. Paris: Plon.

Daintith, Terrence. 1982. Legal Analysis of Economic Policy. Florence: European University Institute, Working Paper no. 27.

De la Serre, Françoise. 1974. L'Europe des Neuf et le conflit israélo-arabe. *Revue Française de Science Politique* 24, no. 4 (August): 801–12.

Elazar, Daniel. 1979. *Federalism and Political Integration*. Lanham/New York/London: University Press of America/Jerusalem Center of Public Affairs.

Elazar, Daniel. 1979. *Self Rule—Shared Rule*. Lanham/New York/London: University Press of America/Jerusalem Center of Public Affairs.

The EEC and the Middle East Peace Process. 1979. London: Institute of Jewish Affairs. I.J.A. Research Report.

European Stance on the Palestinian Issue. 1977. London: Institute of Jewish Affairs. I.J.A. Research Report.

Garfinkle, A. 1981. Europe and America in the Middle East: A New Coordination? *Orbis* 25, no. 3 (Fall): 631–48.

Geiss, Imanuel. 1967. The Germans and the Middle East Crisis. *Midstream* 13, no. 9 (November): 3–9.

Giersch, Herbert, ed. 1980. *The Economic Integration of Israel in the EEC.* Tubingen: J. C. B. Mehr.

Girmont, J. 1979. L'Europe doit-elle avoir une politique arabe? *Revue de Defense Nationale* (August–September): 1256–66.

Goodwin, G. L. 1973. A European Community Foreign Policy. *Journal of Common Market Studies* 12, no. 1 (September): 7–27.

Greilsammer, Ilan. 1976. Theorizing European Integration in Its Four Periods. *Jerusalem Journal of International Relations* 2, no. 1: 129.

Greilsammer, Ilan. 1981. *Israël et l'Europe; une histoire des relations entre la Communauté européene et l'Etat d'Israël.* Lausanne: Centre de Recherches Européenes.

Halpern, Ben. 1979. To Revamp a Party System. *Jerusalem Quarterly*, no. 87 (Summer): 127–44.

Hubert, A. 1977. Le dialogue Euro-Arabe, un parcours d'obstacles. *Revue du Marché Commun* no. 212: 520–27.

Huntzinger, Jacques. 1978. The French Socialist Party and Western Relations. In *The Foreign Policies of West European Socialist Parties*, ed. Werner J. Feld. New York: Praeger.

Jobert, Michel. 1974. *Mémoires d'avenir.* Paris: Grasset.

Kauper, Peter-Jan. 1982. Community Sanctions against Argentina: Lawfulness under Community and International Law. In *Essays in European Law and Integration*, eds. D. O'Keete and H. G. Schermers. Deventer: Klumer.

Kitzinger, Uwe. 1973. *Diplomacy and Persuasion.* London: Thames and Hudson.

Kolodziej, Edward A. 1974. *French International Policy under De Gaulle and Pompidou: the Politics of Grandeur.* Ithaca: Cornell University Press.

Lieber, Robert J. 1976. *Oil and the Middle East War, Europe in the Energy Crisis.* Cambridge: Harvard University Press.

Mac Bride, S., et al. 1983. *Israel in Lebanon.* London: Ithaca Press.

Oliver, Covey. 1974. The Enforcement of Treaties by a Federal State. Vol. 141 (I) *RDC*, p. 333.

Pescatore, Pierre. 1979. External Relations in the Case-Law of the Court of Justice of the European Communities. Vol. 16. *Common Market Law Review* p. 615.

Pescatore, Pierre. 1982. Preface. In *Courts and Free Markets*, Terrence Sandalow and Eric Stein. Oxford: Oxford University Press.

Revue Française de Science Politique 14, no. 4 (April), 1974.

Ronen, Dov. 1979. *The Quest for Self-Determination.* New Haven and London: Yale University Press.

Serfaty, Simon, ed. 1979. *The Foreign Policies of the French Left.* Boulder, Colorado: Westview Press.

Silvestri, Silvano. 1972. Italy's Mediterranean Role. *Lo Spettatore Internationale* 7, no. 2 (April–June): 87–94.

Stein, Eric. 1983. European Political Cooperation as a Component of the European Foreign Affairs System. 43 *Zeitschaft für ausländer Rechte* 49.

United Nations General Assembly. August 1982. *Documents of the 26th Meeting of the Extraordinary Session of the United Nations General Assembly.*

Van Wel, Gunther. 1976. Le développement d'une politique commune des Neuf au Proche-Orient. *Politique étrangère*, no. 2: 105–12.

Vincineau, Michel. 1973. La position belge sur la crise du Moyen-Orient. *La Revue Nouvelle* (Brussels) 27 (April): 446–50.

Vogel, Rolf, ed. 1967. *Deutschlands Weg Nach Israel.* Stuttgart: Seewald Verlag.

Von den Gablentz, Richard. 1979. Luxembourg Revisited or the Importance of European Political Cooperation. *Common Market Law Review* 16: 685.

Weiler, Joseph. 1981. The Community System: The Dual Character of Supra-nationalism. *Yearbook of European Law* 1: 267.

Weiler, Joseph. 1982. The European Parliament and its Foreign Affairs Committees. Padova: Cedam, New York: Oceana.

Weiler, Joseph. 1983. The External Legal Relations of Non-Unitary Actors: Mixity and the Federal Principle. In *Mixed Agreements*, eds. D. O'Keefe and H. G. Schermers. Deventer: Kluxer.

Wheare, K. C. 1963. *Federal Government.* Toronto: O.U.P.

Newspapers and Periodicals

Agence Belga
Akhbar-Ouroubyia-Arabia (Brussels)
Bulletin of the European Community
Combat
Daily Express
Daily Telegraph
D'Letzeburger Land
Europe
Financial Times
France-Soir
Guardian
International Herald Tribune
Irish Press
Irish Times
Jerusalem Post
Jewish Chronicle
Jewish Telegraph Agency
La Cité
La Dernière Heure
La Libre Belgique
Le Figaro
Le Matin
Le Monde
Le Nouveau Journal

Le Nouvel Observator
Le Peuple
Le Quotidien de Paris
Le Republicain Lorrain
Le Soir
L'Humanité
Libération
Middle East International
Scotsman
Times (London)
Tribune Juive

Index